THE APOCALYPSE
OF EZRA

(II ESDRAS III–XIV)

TRANSLATED FROM THE SYRIAC TEXT,
WITH BRIEF ANNOTATIONS

BY

G. H. BOX, M.A.

LECTURER IN RABBINICAL HEBREW, KING'S COLLEGE, LONDON
HON CANON OF ST ALBANS

WIPF & STOCK · Eugene, Oregon

Wipf and Stock Publishers
199 W 8th Ave, Suite 3
Eugene, OR 97401

The Apocalypse of Ezra (II Esdras III-XIV)
Translated from the Syriac Text, with Brief Annotations
By Box, G. H. and Oesterley, W. O. E.
Softcover ISBN-13: 978-1-6667-9085-6
Hardcover ISBN-13: 978-1-6667-9092-4
eBook ISBN-13: 978-1-6667-9093-1
Publication date 9/2/2021
Previously published by SPCK, 1917

This edition is a scanned facsimile of
the original edition published in 1917.

EDITORS' PREFACE

THE object of this series of translations is primarily to furnish students with short, cheap, and handy text-books, which, it is hoped, will facilitate the study of the particular texts in class under competent teachers   But it is also hoped that the volumes will be acceptable to the general reader who may be interested in the subjects with which they deal   It has been thought advisable, as a general rule, to restrict the notes and comments to a small compass , more especially as, in most cases, excellent works of a more elaborate character are available   Indeed, it is much to be desired that these translations may have the effect of inducing readers to study the larger works

Our principal aim, in a word, is to make some difficult texts, important for the study of Christian origins, more generally accessible in faithful and scholarly translations

In most cases these texts are not available in a cheap and handy form.   In one or two cases texts have been included of books which are available in the official Apocrypha , but in every such case reasons exist for putting forth these texts in a new translation, with an Introduction, in this series

W. O E OESTERLEY.
G H. BOX

INTRODUCTION

THE Fourth Book of Ezra—or, as it appears in
our official Apocrypha, 2 Esdras—is, in the form in
which it appears in our Bibles, an enlarged book.
The original work, which forms the Apocalypse proper,
consists of chapters III –XIV of 2 Esdras, and in
the Oriental Versions these chapters form the complete Book   That is to say, chapters I –II and XV –
XVI of our 2 Esdras do not appear in the Oriental
Versions of the Book at all, they are, in fact, later
additions (probably Christian ones) to the Latin
translation of the Apocalypse

The Apocalypse of Ezra (= 2 Esdras III –XIV) is
extant in a Latin and several Oriental translations
which are all based upon a lost Greek Version, and
this latter, again, upon an original Hebrew text (also
completely lost)

The Apocalypse itself appears to be a composite
work which was redacted in its present form by an
Editor about the year A D 120   The material used by
him and embodied in the Book consists of a Salathiel
Apocalypse (cf III I) which is contained mainly in
chapters III –X of 2 Esdras This work, originally
written in the name of Salathiel (= Shealtiel), the
father of Zerubbabel, who lived through the Exile,
is embodied in practically a complete form in our
Apocalypse   It seems to have been written and
published in Hebrew about the year A D 100   To
it the final Editor appended three pieces derived from
other sources, viz (I) the famous Eagle-Vision (chs.
XI –XII) and (2) the Son of Man Vision (ch XIII)
—both extracted apparently from a Book of Dream-
Visions—and (3) the Ezra-Legend (ch XIV. mainly).

There are, naturally, traces of the final Editor's hand throughout in redactional links and adjustments, and also possibly some extracts from an eschatological source detailing the signs which are to precede the End of the World (iv. 52—v 13*a*, vi 11–29). The whole compilation is parallel with the twin (Syriac) Apocalypse of Baruch, which may have been edited in its final form somewhat later. The importance of both Apocalypses for the study of Jewish and Christian theology is very great, and will be referred to more fully below.

TITLE

It is interesting to note that in the Latin MSS. the additional chapters (i –ii xv.–xvi) are distinguished, as a rule, by a separate enumeration. Different arrangements prevail, but the following is a widely accepted one—

1 Esdras = the Canonical Ezra-Nehemiah
2 Esdras = 2 Esdras 1 –ii of our Apocrypha
3 Esdras = 1 Esdras of our Apocrypha
4 Esdras = 2 Esdras iii –xiv. of our Apocrypha
(*i e.* = our Apocalypse)
5 Esdras = 2 Esdras xv –xvi of our Apocrypha

The Oriental Versions also vary in the titles given to our Book. In the Ethiopic and Arabic it is called *The First Book of Ezra* (cf. also colophon at end of Syriac translation, following xiv 50), the title given at the head of the Syriac translation is : *The Book of Ezra the Scribe, who is called Salathiel* Clement of Alexandria quotes from the lost Greek Version as Ἐσδρας ὁ προφήτης, and this may have been the title of the Book in the (lost) Greek translation

THE ANCIENT VERSIONS

The standard text is, of course, the Latin, and the Latin Version has been preserved in a considerable number of Latin MSS. of the Bible But 4 Esdras is no part of the Latin Bible proper ; it is usually printed

as an Appendix to the Vulgate, and certainly was
prized among readers of the Latin Bible. The Vulgate text, as printed, is very corrupt, but considerable progress has been made during comparatively
recent years in the formation of a critical text [1] The
English reader can see many of these results clearly
set forth by a comparison of the A V. and Revised
Version of the Book in our official Apocrypha.

One striking difference which comes to view in the
R V. is that in chapter vii. a long passage of some
seventy verses is inserted between verses 35 and 36,
which is absent from the A V. This is the famous
Missing Fragment which was absent from all known
Latin MSS of the Book till the late Professor R. L.
Bensly discovered (in 1875) the text in a ninth-
century MS, which was then in the possession of the
communal library of Amiens [2] The passage had
been cut out apparently for dogmatic reasons, but
is extant in all the Oriental Versions

The Latin Version, like the Oriental ones, was
made from the lost Greek Version, and is undoubtedly
very early It was well known to Ambrose of Milan,
who cites freely from it As a whole it is singularly
faithful and literal, and is the most valuable of the
Ancient Versions that have come down to us.

The English translations in the A V. and R.V are,
of course, based primarily upon the Latin text. The
Oriental Versions include a Syriac, Ethiopic, two
Arabic, and an Armenian, and some fragments in
other versions (Georgian, etc) Of these by far the
most valuable is the Syriac, from which the following
translation is made. The Syriac text depends upon
a single MS, the great Ambrosian Bible Codex at

[1] Fritzsche's *Libri Vet Test Pseudepigraphi Selecti* (appended to his *Libri Apocryphi Vet Test Græce*, Leipzig,
1871) marked an advance, *The Fourth Book of Ezra*, ed
by Bensly and James, Cambridge, 1895, is the best available
edition in many ways
[2] Prof Bensly published a valuable edition of this dis-
covery *The Missing Fragment of the Fourth Book of Ezra*
(Cambridge, 1875)

Milan   The text has been published by Ceriani. In the MS our Book is preceded by the Apocalypse of Baruch, and is followed by the canonical books of Ezra and Nehemiah, which are reckoned as a single book, viz *The Second Book of Ezra*   Though our book is not given the title of *The First Book of Ezra*, a colophon at the end of the version says *Ended is the first discourse of Ezra*, which presumably implies such an enumeration   The Syriac Version is, on the whole, singularly faithful, though it betrays occasionally a tendency to amplify

The Ethiopic text was first published in 1820 by Richard Laurence, afterwards Archbishop of Cashel. A critical text, based upon several MSS., was prepared by Dillmann, and published after his death   A French translation of this (by Basset) appeared in 1899   The Ethiopic is much more paraphrastic than the Syriac, but occasionally attests valuable readings.

There are two Arabic Versions (Ar [1] Ar.[2]), and also an Armenian Version, which are of less value   For further details see *E A*, General Introduction

The lost Greek text, on which all the Versions (with the possible exception of the Armenian, which may be based directly on the Syriac), are based, has been reconstructed by Hilgenfeld in his *Messias Judæorum* (pp 36–113)

We cannot here give in detail the arguments which make the existence of a Hebrew original highly probable, if not practically certain.   The scholars who accept the hypothesis include Wellhausen, Charles, Gunkel, and Violet   A Greek original has been upheld by some distinguished scholars of an earlier date, notably Lucke, Volkmar, and Hilgenfeld. The question is fully discussed in the General Introduction to *E A*

SPECIAL IMPORTANCE OF THE BOOK

The Ezra-Apocalypse is of many-sided import-ance. It is a genuine product of Judaism, but of a

Judaism that belonged to an earlier type than that
represented in the Rabbinical Literature, as it has come
down to us   In particular the Salathiel portions
of the Book (contained in chapters iii –x) are of
surpassing interest for the student of the New Testa-
ment.   They betray an almost Pauline sense of the
universality and devastating effects of sin (cf. esp.
iv 30, vii 118), and manifest a pathetic longing
for some efficacious means of salvation (viii. 6)
While he values the Law, and the works of the Law,
and even holds that some few, though not sinless,
may yet secure a sufficiency of merit through works
and faith to gain salvation, our Apocalyptist is yet
acutely conscious of the impotence of the Law as a
redeeming power (ix 36, cf Rom iii 20)   He
discusses with profound emotion the problem of
Israel's relation to the Law, and shows unmistakably
that the orthodox answer fails to satisfy him   This
answer may be summed up as follows   (a) God's
ways are inscrutable (iv 7–11, cf v 35 f), (b) human
intelligence is finite and limited (cf iv 12–32), (c) the
course and duration of the present world have been
pre-determined (iv. 33–43), the decisive moment
will soon arrive (iv 44–50).

All difficulties will be solved by the coming in of
the future Age, which will bring in an entirely new
order   The present corruptible world will be dissolved, and give place to the incorruptible world
and immortality (cf vii 114)

One fundamental difficulty to the Apocalyptist
is the fewness of those who are destined to attain
salvation, and the only answer the angel is able to
give him is that the few are precious, and the many
worthless   This provokes the protest that it would
have been better if man had not been created (vii
62–69), or at least restrained from sinning (vii.
116–126).   Against the inevitable conclusion of pure
legalism the seer confidently appeals to the divine
compassion (vii. 132–140)

It will have become apparent how much akin the

thought of our Apocalyptist is to that of St Paul
The same themes are discussed—the relation of Israel
to the Law, faith and works, the divine *parousia*,
grace, sin and the effects of Adam's sin, the benefit
or otherwise of surviving to the *parousia* Mr. C. W
Emmet in an article on *The Fourth Book of Esdras
and St Paul* [1] has worked out, in an illuminating
way, the parallelism in thought between the two
writers. He says—

> " We have seen how 4 Esdras rests finally
> on the inscrutability of God's ways, based on
> His unchallengeable power as Creator, and on
> His fatherly love for His creation. These are
> precisely the two answers which are combined
> in Romans In ch ix St Paul makes his well-
> known appeal to the absolute authority of God
> as Creator—*Nay but, O man, who art thou that
> repliest against God ?*—using the same familiar
> metaphor of the potter and the clay The perora-
> tion of the section in xi 33 ff emphasizes the same
> principle . *How unsearchable are His judgements,
> and His ways past finding out For who hath known
> the mind of the Lord ? or who hath been His coun-
> sellor ?* On the other hand, in ch viii , in dealing
> with the problem of the sufferings of this present
> time and the final deliverance of creation, he has
> asserted the love of God in Christ as the ground
> of hope and the pledge of the ultimate solution
> (viii. 28 ff , cf v 5) The main difference is
> that he has the historical manifestation of that
> love to which he can point in vindication of his
> argument. The fact that both writers place
> these two principles side by side, and that
> neither explicitly combines them, is certainly
> worth notice."

Mr. Emmet also calls attention to further important
parallels. Both emphasize the contrast between Jacob

[1] Published in the *Expository Times* for September 1916
(pp 551–556).

and Esau, with the same quotation from Malachi
(4 Ezra iii 16, Rom. ix 13), cf. also 4 Ezra vii. 72
and Rom. ii 1-16, 4 Ezra vii 73 f. and Rom. ii. 3 f.,
4 Ezra v 41 and 1 Thess iv 13   All this points
to a common background of thought, and shows
that St. Paul was not so isolated in his Jewish ante-
cedents as is often supposed.   As Mr. Emmet well
says—

> " The author of the Salathiel Apocalypse is
> our best representative of the kind of Jewish
> thought with which St Paul must have been
> in sympathy in his pre-Christian days.   Had
> he not become a Christian, he might have written
> just such another book as 4 Esdras, while our
> unknown author would have surely been a strong
> ' Paulinist,' had he been able to adopt the
> Christian solution of the problems he faced so
> bravely."

The other elements in the Ezra-Apocalypse are
also of high importance.   The Eagle-Vision represents well the political eschatology that was accepted
in Zealot circles ; while the Son of Man Vision (ch. xiii.)
is valuable as a presentation of the Apocalyptic view
of the Heavenly Messiah, the Son of Man.   For its
relation to Daniel and to the Similitudes of the Book
of Enoch reference must be made to full discussions
elsewhere (see e. g. *E.A.*, pp. 280 ff.).

BIBLIOGRAPHY

For a full account of the literature bearing on
the subject, reference must be made to larger works.
Constant reference has been made in the notes that
follow to the writer's edition of the Book· THE EZRA-
APOCALYPSE ; *translated from a critically revised text,*
with critical introductions, notes and explanations;
with a General Introduction to the Apocalypse, and an

Appendix containing the Latin text, by G. H Box (London, 1912) [1]

An important edition of the Latin text has been published in the Cambridge series of *Texts and Studies* (vol III no. 2, 1895) *The Fourth Book of Ezra*, the Latin Version edited from the MSS , by the late R. L Bensly, M A., and Dr Montague Rhodes James. The most recent critical edition is that of Dr Bruno Violet, *Die Esra-Apocalypse*, Part I (Leipzig, 1910), it contains not only a critical edition of the Latin text, but also carefully edited German translations of the Oriental Versions

Another important book is Hilgenfeld's *Messias Judæorum* (1869), which contains the Latin text, Latin translations of the Oriental Versions, and a reconstruction of the lost Greek text

The Syriac text from which the translation that follows has been made directly, was published by Ceriani in his *Monumenta Sacra et Profana*, tom v. pp 44–111.

Of other works important for the study of the Book, the following are among the most valuable and accessible—

The Variorum Apocrypha, edited by C J. Ball (gives A.V. with critical notes)

The monumental edition of the *Apocrypha and Pseudepigrapha* (in English translations, with commentaries), edited by Dr R. H. Charles in 2 vols (Oxford, 1913).

F. C Porter, *The Messages of the Apocalyptical Writers* (London, 1909).

Dr. R H. Charles, *A Critical History of the Doctrine of a Future Life* (London, 1899).

Dr. James Drummond, *The Jewish Messiah* (London, 1877)

Dr. W. O. E Oesterley, *Books of the Apocrypha* (London, 1914).

[1] The same writer has also edited the Book in the second volume of Dr. R. H Charles' *Apocrypha and Pseudepigrapha* (Oxford, 1913).

Reference may also be made to—
The Religion and Worship of the Synagogue, by
W. O. E Oesterley and G H Box (2nd ed , London,
1911), and to the articles " Messiah " and " Eschat-
ology " in *The Jewish Encyclopædia* and the Bible
Dictionaries

SHORT TITLES, ABBREVIATIONS AND SIGNS EMPLOYED

1 Enoch = the Ethiopic Book of Enoch.
2 Enoch = the Slavonic Book of Enoch.
Ap. Bar. = The Syriac Apocalypse of Baruch.
Ps Sol. = The Psalms of Solomon.
L   = the Latin version
E.A.   = *The Ezra-Apocalypse* ed. by G H. Box.

(   ) round brackets enclose something added
(in the translation) but not represented in the Syriac
text.

[   ] square brackets enclose something represented
in the Syriac, but absent from L or the other Versions.

†   † translations based upon an emendation in the
Syriac text are so indicated.

THE BOOK OF EZRA THE SCRIBE, WHO IS CALLED SALATHIEL[1]

VISION I
(III. 1—V. 19).[2]

Introduction (III. 1–3).

III 1 In the thirtieth[3] year of the fall of our city I, Salathiel, who am Ezra, was in Babylon, and lay stretched upon my bed and was troubled, and thoughts were coming up upon my heart,[4] 2 because I saw the desolation of Sion and the wealth of the dwellings[5] of Babylon, 3 and my spirit was sore amazed, and I began to speak to the Most High words of fear.

The First Questions: Whence the Sin and Misery of the World? Is Israel's Punishment just? (III. 4–36)

4 And I said O Lord my Lord,[6] didst not thou speak from the beginning,[7] when thou formedst the

---

[1] This is the title of the Book in the Syriac MS
[2] The numeration of chapter and verse follows the Latin (so E V 2 Esdras)
[3] i e primarily the 30th year after 586 B C (= 556 B C), but typically the 30th year after A D 70 (= A D. 100)
[4] *Thoughts heart*, cf Dan ii 29, iv 5
[5] L and other Versions, *dwellers*
[6] L *O dominator Domine* (R V *O Lord that bearest rule*) = Heb '*ădōnai Yahwe*.
[7] = ἀπ' ἀρχῆς, cf Gen ii 7 f

earth—and that thyself alone—and didst command the dust? 5 And it gave thee Adam, a dead body,[1] and he was the formation of thy hands, and thou didst breathe in him the breath of life and he was living before thee, 6 and thou leddest him into Paradise which thy right hand did plant before ever the earth came [2] 7 And to this one thou didst give the commandment,[3] and he transgressed it, and forthwith thou didst decree upon him death, and upon his generations. And from him were born peoples and tribes and tongues and clans which are without number. 8 And all peoples followed [4] their (own) works, and dealt wickedly and were ungodly before thee—and thou didst not hinder them. 9 But again in (due) time [5] thou didst bring the Flood upon the earth and upon the inhabitants of the world, and thou didst destroy them, 10. and their destruction was alike,[6] and as to Adam (came) death, so to them (came) the death of the Flood 11 Nevertheless thou didst spare one of them [7] with his household—and from him all the righteous are descended [8] 12 And it came to pass when the inhabitants of the earth began to multiply, and multiplied [9] children and peoples and many multitudes, and began again to be ungodly more than the former (generations) [10]— 13. it came to pass that when they practised ungodliness before thee, thou didst choose

[1] R V *a body without a soul*
[2] i e Paradise (= the Garden of Eden) was created before the earth, but according to another view (*Jubilees* ii 7) on the third day   See *E A*, pp 195 ff
[3] Lit *didst command the commandment*
[4] Lit *walked in* (for phrase *walked .   works* cf *Ap. Bar* xlviii 38)
[5] Lit *in the time*, i e appointed, cf iv 37
[6] *Alike*, Lit *together* = Heb *bĕ'aḥath* or *ke'ĕḥād* (cf Jer. x. 8)   They were involved in a common fate (L *in uno*)
[7] L + *Noah* (*Noe*)
[8] Lit *have flowed*
[9] L *there were born*
[10] Cf Ps Sol i 8 (*their transgressions were greater than those of the heathen before them*)

one of them for thyself,[1] whose name was Abraham;
14 and thou didst love him, and thou didst shew
him the consummation of the times, him alone, between thee and him by night [2]; 15. and thou didst
establish with him an everlasting covenant,[3] and
didst promise him that thou wouldest never forsake
his seed 16. And thou gavest him Isaac, and to
Isaac thou gavest Jacob and Esau [4], and thou didst
choose thee Jacob for an heritage,[5] and Esau thou
didst hate [6], and Jacob became a great people [7]
17. And when thou didst bring up his seed from
Egypt [and didst establish with him an everlasting
covenant],[8] and didst bring them to Mount Sinai,

18. Thou didst incline the heavens,
    and didst shake the earth—
    and madest the world †quake†,[9]
    and causedst the deeps to tremble,
    and didst alarm the worlds.[10]

19. And thy glory went through the four gates [11]
of fire and earthquake, and of wind and cold, that
thou mightest give to Jacob's seed the Law,[12] and
to the race of Israel commandments 20. And
yet thou didst not remove from them the evil
heart,[13] that thy Law might yield fruit [14] in them
21 For the first Adam clothed himself with the
evil heart, and transgressed, and was overcome (and

[1] Cf Gen xii 1   [2] Cf Gen xv 9 f
[3] Lit *covenants*; cf Gen xvii 7
[4] Cf Josh xxiv 3 f
[5] *Choose   heritage*; L *segregasti tibi*
[6] Cf Mal 1 2 (*Jacob I loved but Esau I hated*)
[7] Cf Gen xxxii 10 f
[8] Accidentally repeated in the Syr MS from ver. 15
above
[9] Reading (with Violet) *wĕ'anîdtāh* for *wa'ḥadtāh* (= *and
thou didst hold*)
[10] L *sæcula* the universe is meant, cf Heb 1 2
[11] The four gates of the four lowest of the seven heavens
may be meant, cf *E A*, p 14
[12] Cf Deut xxxiii 4
[13] L *cor malignum* cf iv 30 (*grain of evil seed*) and vii
92 (*the evil thought*)
[14] *i e* the fruit of death and condemnation, cf Rom vii 5.

not only so) but also †all† ¹ who were begotten from
him. 22. And the infirmity remained in them, and
(also) the Law, together with the evil root; then
what was good departed, and the evil came ²   23
And the times passed away, and the seasons were
ended, and thou didst raise up for thyself a servant
whose name was David;   24. and thou commandedst
him to build ³ a city for thy name ⁴ [and a House] ⁵
that oblations from thine own might be offered therein ⁶   25 And this was done many years   But the
inhabitants of the city sinned against thee   26 and
did nothing new ⁷ beyond what Adam had done and
all his generations, for they also were clothing themselves with the evil heart.   27. And (so) thou deliver-
edst thy City into the hand of thine enemies.⁸

28 And then I said in my heart · Are then the
inhabitants of Babylon behaving well? And hast
thou for this forsaken ⁹ Sion?   29 And it came to
pass when I came hither ¹⁰ I saw many ungodlinesses
which cannot be numbered, and many iniquities ¹¹
my soul saw this thirty years; and my heart was
perturbed,   30 because I have seen

> how thou dost suffer the sinners,
> and sparest the ungodly,
> and hast destroyed thy people,
> and preserved thine enemies;

¹ So read Syriac text *upon*
² The whole body fell under the dominion of sin, cf
Rom vii 7 f and 20 f
³ David is regarded as the founder of the Holy City,
cf x 46
⁴ *i e* the city called by Jahveh's name, the city of God,
cf Jer xxv 29, Ps xlvi 4, xlviii 1 f
⁵ These words are lacking in L, the addition accords
with 2 Sam. vii 5, 13
⁶ This is the correct reading   A V *incense and oblations*
depends upon a corrupt Latin text
⁷ By a slight alteration of the Syriac text the translation
will run *nothing other than [what Adam]*
⁸ Cf x 23
⁹ This is the right reading   L *dominavit (hath she dominion
over Sion?* R V) is probably corrupt for *abominavit*
¹⁰ *i. e* to Babylon   ¹¹ The other Versions have *sinners*

31. and hast not made known unto any [1] how thy
way may be comprehended [2] Hath Babylon behaved better than Sion? 32. Or knowest thou [3]
any other people more than Israel? Or what tribe [4]
hath believed thy covenant as Jacob hath— 33 they
whose reward is not seen, and whose labour hath not
borne fruit ! For I have gone about [5] through the
peoples and have seen that they are now prosperous
although unmindful of thy commandments

34 But now weigh thou [6] in the balance our iniquities and those of the inhabitants of the world, and
the poise of the scale will be seen to be not inclined [7]
35 Or when have the inhabitants of the world not
sinned before thee? Or what people hath so kept
thy commandments? 36. Men, however, with names [8]
thou mayest find who have kept thy commandments,
but a people [9] thou shalt not find

The Divine Reply ; God's ways are
Inscrutable (IV 1—V. 19)

IV 1 And the angel who had been sent unto me,
whose name was Uriel,[10] answered, 2 and said to

[1] L *nihil nemini* corrupted to *nihil memini* in Vulg = *I
remember nought* (cf A V)
[2] = πῶς καταληφθῇ L *derelinqui via hæc* = *how this way
of thine should be forsaken*, cf E A , p 18
[3] = ἔγνως The other Versions read ἔγνω σε (*Hath any
other nation known thee*, etc)
[4] L *tribes*
[5] Lit *passing I have passed*
[6] " Weighing " sins is a common metaphor in Jewish
literature, cf 1 Enoch xli 1 (of weighing deeds)
[7] Read, with a slight emendation of the Syriac, *which
way it inclines* (for *to be not inclined*), cf L *which way the
turn of the scale inclines* The A V represents a corrupt
Latin text
[8] L *homines per nomina* = *men that can be reckoned by
name* (R V), i e noted individuals
[9] So Ethiopic, the other Versions have pl *nations*
[10] Uriel is mentioned again in ver 36 (Latin), v. 20 and
x \28, and not again in the Bible, cf 1 Enoch xxi 5, 9,
xxvii 2, xxxiii 3, 4

me . Is thy heart so perturbed [1] in [2] this world, and wouldest thou comprehend the way of the Most High ? 3. And I answered and said . Yea, my Lord. And he answered me again, and said to me . Three ways have I been sent to shew thee, and three similitudes to set before thee · 4. if thou canst shew me one of these, I also will shew thee the way which thou longest to see, and I will teach thee why [3] the evil heart (exists). 5. And I answered and said · Speak on, my Lord And he answered and said to me .

> Come, weigh me the weight of the fire,
> or measure the measure [4] of the wind,[5]
> or recall me the day that is past

6. And I said to him   Who of those born is able to do these (things) that thou hast spoken to me, that thou shouldest ask me about all these ?

7. And he said to me   Had I asked thee [and said to thee] [6]

> How many chambers [7] are in the heart of the sea [8] ?
> Or how many springs are in the sources [9] of the deep ?
> Or how many ways are above the firmament ?
> Or what are the outlets of Sheol ?
> Or what are the paths of Paradise [10] ?

8 Thou wouldest have said to me .

> Into the deep I have not descended,
> Nor to Sheol as yet have I descended ,
> Neither to heaven have I ever ascended.[11] [12]

[1] Or *disquieted*
[2] i e regarding (in matters pertaining to) , cf John iii 12
[3] A variant reading in L = *whence comes* (but cf R V)
[4] This is the right reading   L has *flatum* = *blast* (probably a corruption of *satum*)
[5] Cf *Ap Bar* lix 5 (for the whole verse)   [6] Added by Syriac
[7] Lit. *treasuries* , other Versions *habitations*
[8] Cf xiii 3, 25, 51 (and Exod xv 8)
[9] Lit *head*, Heb *rôsh* (= *beginning*, e g Lam iii 19) , R V *fountain head*
[10] i e the heavenly Paradise (the paths leading to)
[11] Cf Deut xxx 12 f , Ps cxxxix 8, Rom x 6 f , Baruch iii 29, 39
[12] The Armenian and Ethiopic add another clause *nor entered (ascended into) Paradise*, but L omits.

9. But now I have not asked thee concerning these,
but concerning the fire, and the wind and the day—
things through which thou hast passed [1] and without
which thou canst not be [2], and thou hast said to
me nothing concerning them

10. And he said to me   Thou art incapable of
understanding [3] the things that grow up with thee [4],
11 how, then, can thy vessel [5] comprehend the way
of the Most High ? For the way of the Most High hath
been created incomprehensible,[6] nor is it possible
that one who is corruptible in a corruptible world
should know the way of him who is incorruptible.

The Dialogue continued ; the Limitations of Mortality are Inexorable, and Protests are Useless (IV 12–21)

12 And when I heard these things I fell upon my
face [7] and said to him   It would have been better
for us if we had not come [8] than,[9] having come, that
we should live in sin and suffer, and not know why we
suffer

13 And he answered and said to me . Once there
went [10] the woods of the trees of the plain, and deliber-

---

[1] Reading *passed* by a slight emendation (altering a point)
= " which you have experienced ", Ethiopic takes the
clause closely with *day* (*day that is past*), cf ver 5
[2] For the thought, cf Wisd ix 16
[3] L. + *thine own things*
[4] *i e* the things that have intermingled with thy **growth**
(man was supposed to be compounded of fire, wind, **earth**
and water)
[5] *i e* the body as the vehicle of the soul or understanding
[6] Lit *in what is not comprehended* (the use of *in* here is a
Hebraism)
[7] L. of these opening words is mutilated and corrupt (cf.
A V)
[8] *sc* into life (cf Matt xviii 8) or " into the world "
(= be born), cf John i 9
[9] Lit *or*, a rendering of the Greek comparative ή
[10] Lit *going they went* (a Hebraism), L reads *I went forth
into a wood* (cf. A V)

ated together [1] and said : 14. Come, let us go (and) make war with the sea that it may recede before us, and we will make us more woods [2] 15. The waves of the sea likewise deliberated together,[1] and said : Come let us go up (and) wage war with the wood of the plain in order that there we make us another place. 16 And the deliberation of the wood was in vain, for the fire came and consumed it , 17. and likewise also the deliberation of the waves of the sea, for the sand stood up and stopped them [3] 18 If then thou hadst been judge of these, which of them wouldest thou have acquitted, and which of them wouldest thou have condemned ? 19 And I answered and said . Both of them have deliberated a vain deliberation , for the land hath been given to the wood, and the place of the sea to bear its waves.

20. And he answered and said to me : Thou hast judged well ! And why hast thou not judged thine own self ? 21. For as the land hath been given to the wood, and the place of the sea to bear its waves , [4] so also those who dwell upon the earth are able to understand only what is upon the earth, and he who [5] is above heaven what is above heaven.

The Dialogue continued ; the Seer's Protests are answered by the Assurance that the New Age will solve all Difficulties (IV. 22–32).

22 And I answered and said   I pray thee,[6] my Lord,[7] wherefore, O my Lord, hath understanding been given me for thought ?   23 For I have not

---

[1] Lit. *deliberated a deliberation*
[2] Or sing *another wood*
[3] Cf. Jer v 22
[4] L *and the sea to its waves*
[5] *He who* (sing), Arabic [2] and Armenian understand plural *they who* , L is ambiguous (*qui super cælos*)
[6] Cf ix 44, x 37
[7] This title is often used in address to the angel (iv. 41, v 34 f., etc)

desired to ask about the way [1] of what is above,
but about those things which pass over us daily
> for [2] Israel is given up to the peoples, [3]
> and the people thou hast loved [4] is given up to
> godless tribes,
> and the holy Law of our fathers is set at nought, [5] ·
> and the written covenants [6] are no more,
24. and we pass from the world as locusts, [7]
> and †our life† [8] is as a breath

We indeed [9] are not worthy that mercies should
come [10] upon us, 25 but what will he do for his great
name which is called upon us? [11] About these things
I have asked

The Answer

26 And he answered and said to me . If thou shalt
be [12] thou shalt see, and if thou live long thou shalt
marvel, because the world is hastening fast to pass
away, [13] 27 for it endureth not to bear what hath
been promised [14] to the righteous, because this world
is full of sighing and many infirmities. [15]

28. For the evil concerning which thou didst ask

---

[1] L *ways*
[2] L *wherefore* ? (= διὰ τί, *for* = διότι)
[3] L + *in obprobrium* (= *for reproach*) or (based on another
reading) *in proprium* (= *for a possession*)
[4] Cf Hos xi 1, Jer xxxi 3, Rom xi 28 and *Ap Bar*
v 1
[5] Or *destroyed* (cf xiv 21 f)
[6] A synonym for the Law, cf Rom ix 4
[7] A figure of swiftness, cf Nah iii 17
[8] Text has *we live* emend to *our life*
[9] Lit *also*
[10] Lit *should be*, L *to obtain mercy*
[11] Cf *Ap Bar* v 1 The expression implies ownership;
cf Is xliii 7, lxiii 19, 2 Chron vii 14, and Ps Sol ix 18
(*And thou didst set thy name upon us, O Lord*)
[12] *sc* alive, so L (*si fueris*), but Ethiop *if thou remain*
(survive) = ἐὰν μένῃς (read by L and Syr ἐὰν μὲν ᾖς)
[13] Cf *Ap Bar* xx 1
[14] L + *in their season* (*in temporibus*).
[15] Cf 1 John v 19

me is sown, and its harvest [1] is not yet come. 29 Unless, therefore, that which is sown be reaped, and the place be removed where the evil is sown, the land where the good is sown [2] cometh not 30. Because that one grain of seed of evil [3] was sown in the heart of Adam from the beginning, and how much fruit [4] of ungodliness hath it begotten until now, and shall yet beget until the harvest [1] come !

31. Do thou now reckon up in thine own mind [5] and see how much fruit of ungodliness one grain of seed of evil that was sown hath produced [6], 32 when, therefore, the ears of the good shall be sown,[7] which are numberless, what a harvest are they destined [8] to produce !

The Dialogue continued ; When shall these Things be ? When the Predestined Conditions are Fulfilled (IV 33-43)

33 And I answered and said : How long and when [9] (shall) these things (be) [10] ?   For few and evil are our years

34 And he answered and said to me : Thou mayest not hasten more than the Most High, for thou art hastening for thine own self, but the Most High for (the sake of) many.[11]

35 For did not the souls of the righteous ask

[1] Or *its threshing out* (the word can mean this), cf L *destrictio ejus = the plucking off of it* (corrupted to *destructio*, see A V), cf for the whole idea the parable of the Sower, Matt xiii
[2] *i e* the new age   [3] Cf iii 20   [4] L omits *fruit*
[5] Lit *compare (estimate) in thine own self* (L *æstima autem apud te*)
[6] Lit *made*
[7] *i e* immediately after the dissolution of the present evil age
[8] = Greek μέλλουσιν
[9] Lit *until when and when*, L *usquequo et quando.*
[10] Come to pass, *these things* = these promised good things
[11] Cf v. 33.

THE APOCALYPSE OF EZRA   27

concerning these things in their chambers,[1] and say :
How long shall we be here ? And when (cometh)
the harvest [2] of our reward ?   36 And the angel
Remiel [3] answered and said to them   Until the
number of those like you be fulfilled ! [4] For
     the Holy One hath weighed [5] the world,[6]
37 and with measure hath he measured the times,
     and by number hath he numbered the seasons,[7]
     neither will he rest [8] nor stir,
     till the number appointed be fulfilled [9]
     38 And I answered and said   O Lord my Lord,[10]
but †behold†,[11] we are all full of ungodliness ! 39 Is
it perchance on our account that the reward of the
righteous is withheld, (on account of)[12] the sins of the
inhabitants of the earth ?
     40 And he answered and said to me   Go and
ask (the woman) who is pregnant if, when she com-
pleteth her nine months, the womb can still hold
the birth within her ?
     41 And I said   It cannot, my Lord
     And he answered and said to me   Sheol [13] and the

---

[1] Lit *treasuries*, i e "treasuries of souls" (cf *Ap Bar*
xxi 23), containing the righteous dead, cf vii 32, 80, 95,
Ap Bar xxx 2
[2] L *floor* (threshing-floor)
[3] i e the archangel Jeremiel who had charge of the souls
of the righteous dead, cf i Enoch xx , see *E A* , p 34 f
[4] Cf Rev vi 11
[5] Lit *weighing hath weighed*   [6] Or *age*
[7] The underlying idea is predestinarian, cf Wisd xi 20,
i Enoch xlvii 3
[8] = ? σιγήσει a corruption of σείσει, L has move (*excita-
bit*)
[9] Cf "That it may please thee shortly to accomplish the
number of thine elect and to hasten thy kingdom "
[10] Here and in v 38, vi 11, vii 17, 58, 75 used in address
to the angel, it is strictly only appropriate to God, and is
elsewhere only so used (so always in *Ap Bar*), cf iii 4 (note)
and *E A* , p 36
[11] So read, Syr text *this*
[12] A word has probably fallen out of the Syriac here (add
mĕtûl)
[13] *Sheol and the chambers of souls*, so Ethiop , but L = *the
chambers of souls in the underworld* (Sheol)   See *E A* , p 37

chambers of souls are like the womb   42 for she who is giving birth maketh haste to escape from the anguish of her giving birth, so also do these hasten to give up what hath been put in them   43 from the beginning   And then shall be revealed to thee concerning the things thou longest to see.

The Dialogue continued ; How the End will come (IV 44–50)

44 And I answered and said . If I have found favour in thy sight, and if it be possible and I am worthy,   45 shew me this also, whether the time that hath passed by us be more than that which is to come ?   46 Because the time that is past I know,[1] but what is future I know not

47. And he answered and said to me   Stand on the right side,[2] and I will shew thee the meaning of the similitude

48 And I stood and saw, and behold ! there passed before me a blazing fiery furnace , [3] and it happened that when the flame had passed by I saw, and behold ! the smoke remained   49 And after this there passed before me a cloud filled with water, and poured down a very violent rain, and when the violence of the rain had passed, there remained in it [4] drops (still)

50 And he answered and said to me · Consider in thyself and see,[5] that as the rain exceedeth the drops, and the fire the smoke, so the measure that is passed is excessive [6] , but there remain the drops and the smoke

[1] Cf *Ap Bar* xxiv 3
[2] ? On the right side of the angel (*i e* the speaker) , cf. *E A* , p 39
[3] Cf Gen xv 17 (seen in a vision as here)
[4] *i e* in the cloud
[5] Cf ver 31 , L *consider for thyself* (*cogita tibi*)
[6] L *superhabundavit*

The Signs which Precede the End (IV. 51— V 13)

51. And I besought [1] him and said Shall I then live [2] until those days, or who [3] shall be in those days ?

52 And he answered and said to me Concerning the signs [4] about which thou didst ask me, I can speak to thee of them in part,[5] but concerning thy life I have not been sent to speak to thee, for indeed I have no knowledge

V. 1 Concerning the signs, however ·
Behold the days come [6] when the inhabitants of the world shall be seized with great panic,
and the portion [7] of truth shall be hidden,
and the land of faith shall be unfruitful [8]

2 And iniquity [and shamelessness] [9] shall be increased [10] above this which thou seest now, and above that which thou hast heard of long ago 3 And this land [11] shall be without stability and untrodden [12] which thou hast seen now to be bearing rule, and they shall see this land laid waste 4 But if the Most High grant thee †life† [13] thou shalt see that (land) after the third (day) [14] in confusion

[1] Or *asked*
[2] L *thinkest thou that I shall live* (so Ar [1])
[3] So L (best MSS), reading *quis*, but Ethiop and Ar *what*, so Vulg
[4] Cf Mark xiii 4 and following verses
[5] *Of them in part*, lit *some of them*, the rest are described in vi 11–28
[6] A phrase borrowed from the prophets, cf for its use here *Ap Bar* xxxix 2, lxx 2
[7] Ethiop *region*, L *way* cf *Ap. Bar* xxxix 6
[8] Cf *Ap Bar* lix 10, Luke xviii 8
[9] So Syr , L omits, cf ver 10
[10] Cf Matt xxiv 12   [11] *i e* the Roman Empire
[12] *i e* disordered and pathless, cf Job xii 24
[13] So read by a slight emendation, Syr text *vision*
[14] = μετὰ τρίτην (sc ἡμέραν), *i e* probably towards the end of the last period of 3½ days, after which Rome's oppression will cease, cf *E A*, p 43, A V *after the third trumpet* is corrupt (*tubam* for *turbatam*)

The Episcopal Theological Seminary of the Southwest
Austin, Texas

> And suddenly shall the sun appear by night,
> and the moon by day; [1]
> 5   and the wood shall distil blood, [2]
> and the stone utter its voice, [3]
> and the peoples shall be in commotion,
> and the air [4] shall be changed;

6 and one [5] whom the many do not set their hopes on shall rule, and the birds shall migrate. [6]

7 And the sea of Sodom shall produce many fish [7], and one shall utter his voice by night whom the many know not, [8] and all shall hear it, 8 and fissures [9] shall be produced in many places, and fire [10] shall be emitted continually, and the desert-beasts shall migrate from their places, and signs from women shall appear, for births shall be born without being completed [11], 9 and in sweet waters salt shall be found, and friends shall suddenly wage war on their friends. [12]

> 10   And then shall wisdom hide herself, [13]
> and understanding withdraw to her chambers [14]—
> (and she shall be sought) [15] by many and not
> found,

[1] One of the wonders worked by Antichrist, cf *Asc Is* iv 5

[2] L *blood shall trickle forth from wood*, cf *Ep Barn* xii 1

[3] Cf Hab ii 11, Luke xix 40

[4] Lit *airs* (= ἀέρες ? corrupt for ἀστέρες), for original reading cf *E A*, p 44

[5] *i e* Antichrist

[6] Birds were supposed to possess supernatural knowledge of coming events

[7] The bitter waters of the Dead Sea in which no fish can live, shall be sweetened and produce fish, cf Ezek xlvii 8 f

[8] A mysterious voice shall be heard, cf Josephus, *War*, VI 5 3, L attaches to previous clause *and* [the sea] *shall make a noise*, etc

[9] = χάσματα, cf Zech xiv 4

[10] Cf *Ap Bar* xxvii 10, lxx 8

[11] *And signs   completed*, this seems to be a paraphrase = L *and women shall bear monsters*

[12] Cf vi 24   [13] Cf *Ap Bar* xlviii 36, Is lix 14–15

[14] Lit *treasuries* L sing *chamber*

[15] A word has fallen out accidentally in the Syr = *and she shall be sought*

and transgression and shamelessness shall multiply upon the earth
11 And one place will ask its neighbour,[1] and will
say to it   Hath Righteousness perchance passed
through [2] thee, or [a man] [3] that practiseth righteousness ?   But that place will answer, No [4]   12. And it
shall be in that time men shall hope and not obtain,
[and shall labour and not find,] [5]
and shall toil and their way shall not be made
sure
13 These signs I have been commanded to tell
thee; but if thou wilt pray again and †weep† [6] as
now, and fast seven days,[7] thou shalt hear greater
things than these.

The Conclusion of the Vision (V. 14–19)

14 And I awoke,[8] and my body trembled greatly,
and my soul was weary as though it would expire [9]
15 But the angel who spake with [10] me took hold of
me and strengthened me and set me up upon my
feet
16 And it came to pass in the second night there
came to me †Phaltiel† [11] the head of the people, and
said to me   Where hast thou been, and why is thy
countenance sad [12] ?   17 Or dost thou not know that
thou hast been entrusted with [13] Israel in the place

---

[1] Lit *what is nigh to it*   [2] Or *by*   [3] L omits *a man*
[4] Lit *will deny*, cf Amos vi 10   [5] Omitted by L
[6] So read (by a slight emendation), Syr text has *supplicate*
[7] This was the regular preparation for the reception of
the divine revelation, four such are referred to in this Book,
cf v 20, vi 35, ix 26, 27, xii 51
[8] *sc* from sleep, the previous vision was a dream-vision
[9] Cf *Ap Bar* xxi 26
[10] Lit *in* or *through*, cf Zech ii 3
[11] The historical reference is uncertain, for the name cf.
2 Sam iii 15   Syr text *Psaltiel*
[12] *Sad* from fasting, cf Matt vi 16
[13] Lit *over*   the seer is the last of the prophets left to the
exiles in Babylon, cf xii 42

of their captivity? 18. Stand up, then, and eat a little bread so that thou do not leave us as (doth) a shepherd his flock in the hand of destructive wolves ! [1] 19 And I said to him . Depart from me and come not nigh unto me until seven days ; and then thou mayest come unto me and I will explain matters to thee. And when I had spoken to him he departed from me.

[1] For the image cf Matt x. 16

VISION II

(V. 20—VI 34)

THE PRAYER OF EZRA [1]

Introduction (V 20–22)

20. And I fasted seven days, sighing and weeping, even as Ramiel [2] the angel commanded me   21. And it came to pass after seven days the thoughts of my heart were again oppressing me [3] greatly   22. And my soul received the spirit of intelligence, and I began again to speak before the Most High these words of supplication and entreaty ·

The Prayer and its Answer (V 23–40)

23 And I answered and said   O Lord my Lord, from all the woods of the earth and the trees thereof thou hast chosen thee one vine [4],   24 and from all the lands of the world thou hast chosen thee one place [5],   25   and from all the deeps of the sea thou hast enlarged for thyself one stream,[6] and from all the

---

[1] This title is prefixed to the following section in the Syriac text

[2] Cf iv 36, the other Versions rightly read here *Uriel*

[3] Cf iii 1

[4] The figures illustrating Israel's choice have been drawn from the O T   For the vine cf Is v 7, Ps lxxx 9, vers 23–27 read like an old Midrash, cf Midrash rab on Cant ii 1 and *Pirke R Eliezer*, ch xix

[5] *i e* the Holy Land   L *pit* (for the vine).

[6] *i e* the Jordan

flowers of the world thou hast chosen thee one flower [1], and from all the cities that have been built thou hast sanctified Sion unto thyself [2], 26 and from all birds that have been created thou hast named for thyself one dove [3], and from all cattle that have been created thou hast selected one sheep [4], 27 and from the multitude of the peoples thou hast brought nigh to thyself [5] one people, and the Law which was approved from among all [6] thou hast given to the people whom thou hast loved

28. And now, O Lord, why hast thou delivered up one unto many, and hast dishonoured the one root [7] above the many, and hast scattered and dispersed thine only one among the many? 29 And those who resist thy commandments have trodden under foot them that have believed thy covenant 30 And if thou didst hate thy people so much,[8] the obligation was that they should be punished with thine own hands.[9]

31 And after I had spoken these words, the angel was sent unto me, that had been sent unto me in the night that was past,[10] 32 and said to me ·

Hear me, and I will inform thee, [Ezra], [11]
look at me, and I will set words before thee.

33 And I answered and said to him Speak on, my Lord And he said to me Art thou perturbed

[1] L *one lily* = Israel, cf Cant ii 2
[2] Cf Ps cxxxii 13
[3] = Israel, cf Ps lxxiv 19, Cant ii 14
[4] Cf Ps lxxix 13
[5] i e appropriated
[6] i e out of all laws the Mosaic was the best, cf Deut. iv 8
[7] Cf 1 Enoch xciii 8 (*race of the Elect root*), Rom xi 17 f
[8] *Didst hate   so much*, Lit *hating didst hate*
[9] i e by famine, pestilence, or earthquake, but not by foreign foes (cf 2 Sam xxiv 13), cf also Ps Sol vii 3, Ecclus ii 18
[10] i e not the night immediately past, some days had elapsed (cf v 20)
[11] Omitted in the other Versions

on account of Israel ? Or lovest thou him more than
he that made him ? [1]

34 And I said No, my Lord ! But I am in sore
pain,[2] and spoke because my reins scourge me [3]
every hour, [4] because I seek to comprehend the
decree of judgement of the Most High, and I would
search out something of his judgement [4]

35 And he said to me Thou canst not And I
said to him Why, my Lord, †am I not able† ? [5] Or
why was I born, and why did not my mother's womb
become my grave,

> that I might not see Jacob's travail,
> and the toil of Israel's seed ? [6]

36 And he answered and said to me ·
> Number me those who are not yet come,[7]
> and gather me the drops [8] that are scattered,
> and make bloom for me the flowers that are
> withered, [9]

37. And open me the chambers [10] that are closed,
> and bring me forth the winds [11] held captive in
> them,
> and shew me the likeness of persons whom thou
> hast never seen,
> or shew me the likeness of a voice,

and then I will inform thee concerning the travail [12]
[and the time] [13] that thou askest to see

[1] Cf viii 47   [2] Lit *being in pain I am in pain*
[3] Cf Ps lxxiii 21 (the reins or kidneys seat of strong
emotion)
[4] For *decree of judgement* L has *way*, and for *something
of his judgement* L has *partem judicii* Syriac here seems
to have a doublet, see *E A*, p 56
[5] So read, by a slight emendation, Syr text *should I not
pray*
[6] Quoted by Clement of Alex, *Stromateis*, iii 16
[7] *i e* the unborn, so L, Ethiop and Ar *the days that
are not yet come*
[8] *i e* the rain-drops, cf iv 50
[9] Cf Ezek xvii 24   [10] Lit *treasuries*
[11] Or *spirits* (the same Heb word = both *wind* and *spirit*),
i e the spirits of the righteous dead, cf iv 35 for the
chambers of the winds cf i Enoch xli 4, Rev vii 1
[12] *i e* ? the painful problem   [13] Added by the Syriac

38 And I said   O Lord, my Lord, who is there who could know these (things) except him who dwelleth not with men ? 39. I, however, am foolish and weak, how should I be able to speak concerning these things which thou hast asked me ?

40 And he said to me   Just as thou art unable to do one of the things that have been mentioned,[1] so thou art unable to find out my judgement or the end of the love which I have promised [2] to my people

The Succession of Generations and the Divine Plan of the World (V. 41–55)

God's Judgement reaches all alike

41 And I said   But, my Lord, behold thou hast made the promise [3] to those who are in the End, but what shall they do who were before us, or we (ourselves), or those who follow us ? [4]

42 And he answered and said to me   I have made my judgement like a crown [5], just as there is no posteriority for the last, so also there is no priority for the first [6]

43. And I answered and said   Couldest thou not then, perhaps have made those who have been and those who are and those who shall be all at once, that thou mightest make known thy judgement quickly ?

44 And he answered and said to me   The creation hasteneth not faster than its Creator, otherwise, indeed, the world could not endure those created in it all at once

45 And I again answered and said   And how (is it) thou hast (just now) said [7] to thy servant that thou wilt verily revive thy creation, which hath been

---

[1] Lit *said*   [2] Or *professed*   [3] Lit *thou hast promised.*
[4] For the problem propounded cf I Thess iv 13 f
[5] So L , Ethiop (Ar [1]) *like a ring*
[6] God's judgement will reach all, those who lived in former ages, and those living in the latest period, at the same time, cf *Ap. Bar* li 13
[7] Viz in ver 42

created by thee, all at once [1] ? If, then, they shall indeed revive all at once, and the creation endure (it), it might even now endure them being (present) all at once

46. And he answered and said to me . Ask the womb of a woman, and say unto it [2]. If thou bearest ten (children) why dost thou bear them at different times [3] ? Demand, therefore, from it [2] that it [2] produce its ten at once [4]

47. And I said It cannot, my Lord, except at (different) times.[3]

 48 And he said to me . I also have made the earth the womb of those who come upon it at (different) times [3] 49 For just as the child doth not bear, (nor) she that is aged any more, so also have I ordered the world that I have created [5]

The Earth is grown Old and its Offspring Degenerate

50 And I asked him and said Now [6] that thou hast given me the way,[7] I would speak before thee. Our mother [Sion],[8] of whom thou hast spoken to me, is she really, [my Lord],[8] still young, or already approaching old age ? [9]

51 And he answered and said to me Ask (a woman) that beareth, and let her tell thee , 52 say to her. Why are those whom thou bearest now (not) [10] like

---

[1] *i. e* at the last Judgement
[2] *i e* the womb, or *unto her* (the woman), and so throughout the passage
[3] Lit *at time and time*
[4] Lit *that it produce them in their (whole of) ten*
[5] Ethiop + κατὰ καιρὸν (*according to season*) The earth in its extreme youth brought forth no human inhabitants, neither will it do so in extreme old age
[6] Lit *from now*
[7] *i e* opened up a way, freely given opportunity
[8] Added by Syriac, other versions omit   [9] Cf iv 33 f
[10] It is necessary to supply the negative particle, which has accidentally fallen out of the Syriac MS , so the other Versions

the former ones, but inferior in size [1] ?   And   53 she
also shall say to thee . those born in the vigour of
youth are of one fashion , and those born in old age,
when the womb is diminished, are of another   54 Do
thou also look and see that ye are inferior in size to
those who preceded you ,   55 they also that come
after you shall be inferior to you, because the creation
hath already grown old,[2] and   the vigour of her
youth is past.

The End mediated by God alone (V 56—VI. 6)

56. And I answered and said : I beseech thee, my
Lord, if I have found favour before thee, tell thy
servant by whom [3] thou wilt visit thy creation.

VI. 1 And he answered and said to me : The
beginning by the hand of man,[4] but the end by mine
own hands

> For [as] [5] before the land of the world existed,
>   and before the outgoings of the world [6] were
>   standing,
>   and before the weights of the winds [7] blew ,
> 2. and before the voice of the thunders was
>   heard,
>   and before the lightning-flashes did shine ,
>   and before the land of Paradise was founded,

[1] L *inferior in stature (minores statu)*
[2] For the idea cf xiv 10, 16 , *Ap Bar* lxxxv 10, Ambrose,
de bono mortis, x ; and see further *E A* , p 63
[3] A variant reading (Ethiop Ar) is *on account of whom*,
perhaps a tendency alteration made to meet Christian objec-
tions , see *E A* , p 64
[4] Or *by the hand of the Son of Man*, but where *the Son of
Man* is a proper name in the Gospels the word for *son* is
defined (*bĕreh*), here, however, it is not (*bar* alone), and
bar nasha = man   The text is probably out of order   L
has a lacuna after *beginning* down to *existed*   Volkmar
restores the missing line thus   *the beginning of the terrestrial
world was by me myself   For before the earth and the universe
were created* [*and before the outgoings of the world*, etc].
[5] This is added by Syriac , omit
[6] Cf 1 Enoch xxxiv
[7] *i e* the heavy winds , cf *Ap Bar* lix 5

3 and before the beauty of the flowers [1] was
   seen,
   and before the power of the commotions [2] was
    strengthened,
   and before the numberless armies of angels were
    gathered,
4 and before the height of the air [3] was up-
   lifted,
   and before the measures [4] of the firmaments
    were named [5],
   and before the footstool of Sion was strength-
    ened, [6]
5 and before the years that are present were
   sought out,
   and before the follies of present-day [7] sinners
    were conceived,
   and before those who have gathered for them-
    selves the treasures of faith were sealed [8]—
6. then (it was) I thought, [9] and all these things came
into being [10] by mine own hand alone and not by the
hands of another [11]

The Parting Asunder of the Times
(VI. 7–10)

7 And I answered and said What is the dividing
asunder of the times ?   Or when is the end of the first
age, or what the beginning of the second ? 8. And

---

[1] i e of Paradise   [2] i e earthquakes   [3] Lit. airs
[4] i e measured spaces, i e divisions into which the
heavens were separated
[5] The seven heavens have each a special name, cf E A,
p 65
[6] Or made firm, i e established, appointed (the A V or
ever the chimneys in Sion were hot rests upon a corrupt text).
For God's footstool cf Ps xcix 5, cxxxii 7, Lam ii 1, etc.
[7] Lit now
[8] For the " sealing " of the faithful cf Rev vii 4
[9] Or considered   [10] Lit were
[11] L + as also the end through me alone and none other :
the Oriental Versions omit this clause for dogmatic (Christian)
reasons

he answered and said to me From Abraham until Abraham [1] From Abraham [was begotten Isaac, and from Isaac] [2] (were) [3] begotten Jacob and Esau, and the hand of Jacob was holding Esau's heel [4] 9 The heel of the first (is) Esau, and the hand of the second (is) Jacob [5], 10 for the first [6] of a man is his hand, and the end of a man is his heel Thus between heel and hand do thou seek nought else, O Ezra !

The Signs of the Last Time and the End
(VI 11–28)

11. And I answered and said O Lord my Lord : If I have found favour in thy sight, [7] 12 make known to thy servant the end [8] of the signs, which thou hast made known to me †in part† [9] in the night that is past

13 And he answered and said to me Stand up upon thy feet, [10] and thou shalt hear a loud voice [11] 14. And it shall be that if the place whereon thou standest be greatly shaken, [12] 15 while speech is made with thee, thou shalt not be terrified, because the speech is concerning the report of the End, and the foundations of the earth shall understand 16 that the speech is concerning them ; and they shall tremble

---

[1] Possibly the underlying Greek is ἀπὸ τοῦ 'Αβραὰμ ἕως ʳτῶν τοῦ 'Αβραάμ (Hilgenfeld), i e from Abraham to his immediate descendants The new age will follow this *immediately* without a break

[2] L and other Versions omit reading *from A (were) begotten Jacob and Esau* Syriac may be right

[3] Text has sing *was (begotten)*, the twins being regarded as one birth

[4] L + *from the beginning* (so Ar [1])

[5] So Syr rightly. L has *For Esau is the end of this world, and Jacob is the beginning of it that followeth* (R V)

[6] i e the beginning   [7] L + *I beseech thee.*

[8] i e the last

[9] So emend Syriac to read (*part*) *of them* instead of *from me*

[10] Cf Ezek ii 1, Dan vii 4

[11] Cf Exod xix 16   [12] Lit *shaking shake*

and quake,[1] for they feel that their end (is being) changed [2]

17 And it came to pass that when I heard I stood upon my feet, and I heard, and lo ! a voice of one speaking,[3] and his [4] voice was as the voice of many waters [5] 18 And he [6] said

Behold the days come,[7] and it shall be,

when I am drawing nigh to visit the dwellers upon earth,

19 and when I am about to require at the hands of evil-doers   [8]

and when the humiliation of Sion shall be complete ,[9]

20 and when this world [10] is about to be sealed,[11]

which is about to pass away—

these signs I will do   the books [12] shall be opened before the face of the firmament, and all shall see [my judgement] [13] together

[14] [21 And children one-year old shall speak and utter their voice [15] , and pregnant women untimely shall bear children at three and four months, and they shall live and dance.   22 And suddenly †unsown† [16] places shall be found sown,[17] and full storehouses shall suddenly be found empty][14]

---

[1] Lit *be moved* or *shaken*   [2] Participle in Syr
[3] Or *a voice speaking*   [4] Or *its*
[5] Cf Ezek 1 24, Rev 1 15, xiv 2, xix 6   The Divine Voice is meant
[6] Or *it* (the voice)
[7] A common introductory phrase, especially in the prophets (cf Amos viii 11, ix 13), and adopted by Apocalyptic writers (cf *Ap Bar* xx 1, xxiv 1, etc)
[8] A word seems to have fallen out = *their iniquity* (cf L)
[9] The fall of Jerusalem is a definite step towards the End, cf *Ap Bar* xx 2   [10] Or *age*
[11] i e closed up like a document that is sealed
[12] i e the celestial records of the deeds of the righteous and wicked, cf Dan vii 10, Rev xx 12, *Ap. Bar* xxiv 1
[13] So Syr , the other Versions omit (or supply *them* or *me*)
[14] Probably vers 21–22 are misplaced, and belong between vers 8 and 9 of ch v , see *E A* , p 75
[15] Cf *Jubilees*, xxiii 25   [16] So emend, text " unsowing."
[17] Cf Enoch lxxx. 2 , *Jubilees*, xxiii 18

23. and the trumpet [1] shall call with a loud sound,
which all shall hear suddenly and be affrighted.
24 And it shall come to pass in that time friends
shall war with their friends as enemies, (so) that the
earth shall be amazed with its inhabitants, and
the outgoings of the springs shall stand (still) without
running [2] three hours [3]

25. And it shall be (that) every one who surviveth [4]
all these things of which I have told thee beforehand,
he shall live and see my deliverance [5] and the end of
the [6] world   26 And then shall he see the men who
have been taken up, who have not tasted death since
their birth.[7]   And the heart of the inhabitants of
the earth shall be transformed, and changed into a
different mind [8]

27. For evil is blotted out
    and deceit extinguished,
28. and faith blossometh,
    and corruption is overcome;
    and truth appeareth which hath remained
        without fruit (so) many years

29 And it came to pass, while he [9] spake with
me, that behold, little by little, the place on which I
was standing shook.

---

[1] i e the trumpet which ushers in the last judgement (cf
Sibyll. Or. iv 173 f), elsewhere it is associated with the
awakening of the sleeping dead (I Cor xv 52, I Thess iv
16), see further *E A*, p 75
[2] Cf. Ps Sol xvii 21, *Assumpt Moses*, x 6, *Test XII
Patr Levi* IV
[3] Ar [2] *years*
[4] Cf. *Ap Bar* xxxii 1, lxxi 1, xxix 2, I Thess iv 15,
Mark xiii 13, and in this Book ix 8, xiii 16–24, 26, 48
[5] i e. the Messianic salvation, cf *e g* Luke ii 30
[6] L *my*
[7] i e the men removed from earth without dying, especially
Enoch and Elijah (also, in our Book, Ezra, cf xiv 9), see
L A, p 77 f
[8] Cf **Mal** iv. 6 (Heb iii. 24) of Elijah
[9] Or *it* (the Divine Voice).

The Conclusion of the Vision (VI. 30–34)

30 And he said to me . These things [1] I came to make known to thee this night   31 If, therefore, thou wilt again supplicate and fast seven days more, I will reveal to thee the things greater than these [1] 32. Because thy voice hath surely been heard with the Most High; for the Mighty One [2] hath seen thy purity,[3] yea [4] the holiness [5] which hath been thine from thy youth. 33. And therefore hath he sent me to reveal to thee all these things   [6] And he said [6] to me : Take heart, and fear not !   34 And be not hasty to think evil [7] of [8] former times, lest inquisition come upon thee in the last times ! [9]

[1] i e the content of the previous Vision L adds at end of ver 31 per diem, which probably represents something which should belong to following verse (? pridem), cf E A , p 80

[2] Cf ix 45

[3] L thy rectitude

[4] L + hath marked (providit)

[5] L chastity (pudicitiam), chastity, like fasting, intensifies the power of prayer, and prepares the way for a revelation (cf i Enoch lxxxiii 2)

[6] L and to say

[7] i e indulge in idle thoughts

[8] Lit concerning

[9] See E A , p 81

VISION III

(VI 35—IX. 25)

Introduction (VI. 35–37)

35 And it came to pass after this I wept and fasted seven days that I might fulfil the three weeks [1] which had been commanded me. 36. And it came to pass in the eighth night that lo ! my heart was again moved within me, and I began to speak before the Most High , 37. because my spirit was greatly inflamed,[2] and my soul was on fire [3]

The Problem ; If the World was created for Israel, why is Israel disinherited ? (VI. 38–59) [4]

38 And I said   O Lord [my Lord],[5] thou didst indeed [6] speak at [7] the beginning of thy [8] creation on the first day, and didst command [9] that heaven and earth should be,[10] and thy Word,[11] [O Lord],[12] perfected the work.   39 And the Spirit [13] was then hovering,

[1] Only two have been mentioned, viz one here, and one before the second Vision, there seems to have been one originally before Vision I, cf *E A* , p 82
[2] Cf Ps xxxix 3 , Luke xxiv 32
[3] L *was in distress (anxiabatur)*
[4] Probably an old Jewish Midrash on the works of creation underlies this, see *E A* , p 83
[5] So Ethiop Ar [1], L omits.   [6] Lit *speaking*
[7] Lit *from*   [8] L *the*
[9] Lit *say*   [10] Cf Gen 1 1
[11] Note this hypostasizing use of *Word* developed from such passages as Ps xxxiii 6, cf Heb xi 3 , 2 Pet iii 5
[12] Omitted by the other Versions
[13] Cf Gen 1 2

and darkness (was) veiling [1] and [2] silence of the voice; and the voice [2] of man was not yet   40 Then thou didst command that a ray of light [3] should come forth out of thy treasuries in order that thy works might become visible

41. And on the second day again thou didst create the spirit [4] of the firmament and didst command it to make a division between the waters and the waters, [5] in order that a portion of them might ascend on high and the other portion remain beneath.

42 And on the third day [6] thou didst command the waters to be gathered together to one of the seven parts [7] of the earth, but six parts thou didst dry up and reserve that some of [8] them might be serving before thee and be both ploughed and sown [9]   43 But thine own Word went forth, and immediately the work was done

44 For then straightway [10] there sprang forth
    fruits many, innumerable,
    and sweet in their tastes, of every sort, [11]
    And flowers which in their forms were unlike
        one another, [12]
    [and trees which in their appearance were
        dissimilar,] [13]

---

[1] L [tenebræ] circumferebantur

[2] L silentium, sonus vocis   for silence of the voice (or sound) cf 1 Kings xix 12, R V marg a voice of gentle stillness   For the conjunction of silence and darkness cf E A, p 84

[3] i e heavenly (not created) light, it was afterwards withdrawn, cf E A, p 85

[4] i e angel   [5] Cf Gen 1 6 and see Jubilees, ii 4

[6] Cf Gen 1 9-13, Jubilees, ii 5-7

[7] Clement of Alex, Recognitions, ix 26, Philo Mund opif 34-36

[8] Lit from

[9] The cultivation of the soil is man's destiny and duty from the beginning, cf Gen ii 15, Ps civ 14, and see E A, p 86 f   Some mention of the creation of Paradise might be expected here

[10] Lit suddenly, L subito

[11] i e exquisitely varied in taste   [12] L of inimitable colour.

[13] So Ethiop Ar.[1], but L omits

and odours which in their scents [1] were in-
definable [2]
These came into being on the third day.

45 And on the fourth day thou didst command,
and there came into being the shining sun, and the
light of the moon, and the order of the stars [3], 46
and thou didst command them to serve man [4] who
was about to be formed by thee.

47. And on the fifth day [5] thou didst give command
to the seventh part, where the waters were, that
beasts and birds and fishes should come forth, and
they came into being [6] 48 The dumb and lifeless [7]
waters were producing that in which there was life,[8]
that from these the generations might declare thy
wonders [9] 49 And then thou didst reserve two
creatures [which thou hadst created] [10], and thou
didst call the name of the one Behemoth, and the
name of the other thou didst call Leviathan [11] 50
And thou didst separate them, the one from the other,
because that moist seventh part [12] was unable to
contain them [13] 51 And thou didst give to Behemoth
one of the parts which had been dried up on the third
day, that he might dwell there, where (are) a thousand
mountains [14], 52 but to Leviathan thou didst give

[1] Lit *odours*
[2] Lit *unsearchable*   This description may have originally
been one of the beauties of Paradise, see *E A*, p 88
[3] Astronomy was a subject of much interest in Apocalyptic
circles, see, *e g*, 1 Enoch lxxii –lxxxii
[4] Cf Clement of Alex, *Recognitions*, v 29
[5] Cf Gen 1 20–23, *Jubilees*, 11 11–12, 2 Enoch xxx 7
[6] Lit *and they were* LXX in Gen 1 20 has *and it was so*
at end of verse
[7] Lit *without soul*
[8] Or *soul* (Heb *nefesh*), the vital principle
[9] Cf Ps xxvi 7, cv 2   [10] Other Versions omit
[11] For the myth of Behemoth and Leviathan cf *E A*,
pp 90–92
[12] *That moist seventh part* = L *where the water was gathered
together*
[13] Both were originally sea-monsters
[14] Cf Ps l 10 (*Behemoth* [E V *cattle*] *upon a thousand
hills*)

one of the seven parts of the moisture and thou hast reserved them to be food for whom thou wilt and when thou wilt [1]

53 And on the sixth day [2] thou didst command the earth that it should bring forth before thee cattle and beasts [3] and creeping things And over these [however] thou didst appoint Adam as leader over all the works [4] that thou didst create antecedently, and from him are we, the people whom thou hast chosen

55 All this, however, I have spoken before thee, O Lord [my Lord], [5] because thou hast said that for our sakes thou didst create this [6] world [7], 56 but as for the rest of the peoples who are descended [8] from Adam, thou hast said that they are nothing,[9] and hast likened them unto spittle,[10] and to a drop from a bucket hast thou likened their abundance [11] 57 And now, O Lord, behold, these peoples which are reputed as nothing [behold] lord it over us and crush [12] us ! 58 But we, thy people, whom thou hast honoured and hast called the first-born [13] and only (begotten),[14] near and beloved (one) [15]—lo ! we are given up into their hands 59 And if for our sakes the world was created, why do we not inherit our world ? How long (shall) these things (be) ?

[1] Cf *Ap Bar* xxix 4, where it is made clear that the righteous will devour the monsters at the Messianic banquet. For the modification here see *E A*, p 90

[2] Cf Gen 1 24–28, *Jubilees*, 11 13–14, 2 Enoch xxx 8 f

[3] *i e* beasts of prey

[4] Cf *Ap Bar* xiv 18

[5] Other Versions omit   [6] L *the*

[7] For this doctrine cf vii 11, *Assumpt Moses*, 1 1, 2, *Ap Bar* xv 7, and see further *E A*, p 93 f

[8] Lit *begotten*

[9] Cf Isa xl 17 (Dan iv 35 or 32)

[10] Cf Isa xl 15 in LXX, which read *rōḳ for dōḳ*—a Hebrew text apparently followed here

[11] *i e* wealth, superfluity

[12] L *devour*

[13] Cf Exod iv 22, Ps lxxxix 27 (28), Ecclus xxxvi 12

[14] Cf Ps Sol xviii 4, and see *E A*, p 96

[15] Cf Jer xii 7, Rom xi 28, *Ap Bar* xxi 21

The Debate resumed ; The present Corrupt Order makes the Path to future Felicity narrow and difficult (VII. 1-25)

1. And it came to pass after I had finished speaking these words, lo ! there was sent unto me the angel [1] that had been sent unto me on former nights. 2 And he said to me · Stand up, Ezra, and hear the words that I have come to say to thee   And I said to him . Speak on, my Lord !

3 And he answered and said to me . If a sea be set [2] in a wide place, so that it is broad and un-limited, 4 but its entrance is set [2] in a narrow place, so that it is like a river , 5 and [3] if a man desire to enter upon the sea, and to behold it and master it [4]—if then he do not pass through the narrow, how shall he be able to come into the broad ?

6 [Hear] [5] again another thing [6]   There is a city that is built and set [7] in a large place of the valley,[7] and that city is full of many good things , 7 and its entrance is narrow and set on a height,[8] so that there is fire on the right hand, and on the left deep waters ,

8. and a single path is set between these two, between the fire and the waters, so that that path only sufficeth for a man's footstep alone.   If now that city be given [9] for an inheritance, unless that heir pass through the danger that is set,[10] how shall he be able to receive his inheritance ?

[1] i e Uriel   [2] = Gk κεῖται   [3] Lit but (= δὲ)
[4] Lit be lord over it   so L (dominari), possibly due to mis-translation of Heb (hirdōth for lāredeth = to go down on, navigate), see E A p 100
[5] L omits
[6] i e another illustration
[7] L in loco campestri = ἐν τόπῳ πεδινῷ, cf Luke vi 17 : the Syriac may be rendered valley or plain
[8] L on a steep (in præcipiti)   For the narrow (as opposed to the broad) way cf. Matt vii 13, 14, and for the difficult way leading to a broad plain cf Ps lxvi 12 (reading into a spacious place)
[9] To a man should be added (so other Versions)
[10] Add before (him), a word may have fallen out.

10 And I said to him   It is indeed so, my Lord !
And he answered and said to me   So also is Israel's
portion, 11 for, for their sakes I made the world and
when Adam transgressed my commandments, that
which had been made was condemned[1] 12 And
on this account the entrances of this [present][2]
world became narrow and full of sighing and travail
and many dangers, and much weariness [together
with sicknesses and pains][3], 13 but the entrances
of that future world are broad and care-free,[4] and
produce fruits that do not die[5] 14 Unless, then, the
living pass through the tribulation and these evils,
they shall not be able (to receive)[6] what has been
kept[7] for them
    15 But now
        wherefore art thou perturbed that thou art
        corruptible,
        and why art thou moved that thou art mortal ?[8]
16 And why hast thou not considered what is to
come, but (only) what is present ?[9]
    17 And I answered and said   O Lord, my Lord,
but lo ! thou hast ordained in thy Law[10] that the
righteous are to inherit[11] these things, but the ungodly are to perish[11] 18 The righteous, therefore, endure[12] well the tribulations[13] because they
hope [to inherit][14] the spacious (things),[15] but the
ungodly bear the tribulations[13] and do not see the

[1] Cf *Ap Bar* xxiii 4, Rom viii 20 Adam's sin was
devastating in its effects
[2] Added by Syriac
[3] Apparently an addition by the Syriac, for the original
form of the sentence see *E A*, p 102
[4] L. *Safe* (*securi*)
[5] Fruits of immortality, cf Prov xii 28
[6] A corresponding word seems to have fallen out of the
Syriac
[7] L lit *set*   [8] Do not brood over death and mortality
[9] The New Age will solve these riddles
[10] Cf Deut viii 1   [11] Participle in Syr. (*are inheriting*, etc)
[12] L reads future tense (rightly)
[13] Or *narrow things*   [14] Other Versions omit.
[15] For the sentiment cf *Ap Bar* xiv 12
    D

spacious (things) !   19. And he answered and said to
me :

> Thou art not (wiser) [1] than God,
>   nor of greater understanding than the Most
>   High !

20 Therefore let the many who have come [2] perish
[3] on the ground that through them the Law hath been
despised which was established by me [3] !   21. For
God gave a commandment to them that have come,[2]
then when they came,[2] as to what they should do and
live, and what they should observe and not be
punished [4]

> 22. But they resisted and obeyed him not,[5]
>   and they devised for themselves vain thoughts,
>   and they added [6] for themselves treacheries of
>   apostasy,
> 23 and beyond all this they affirmed that the Most
>   High existeth not,[7]
>   and did not recognize [8] his ways !
> 24 And his Law they despised,
>   and his covenants they †denied†,[9]
>   and believed not his commandments,
>   and spurned his works [10]
> 25 Wherefore, O Ezra,
>   empty things for the empty,
>   and full things for those who are full ! [11]

---

[1] L *a judge* (*above*) · probably a word (= *wise*) has fallen
out of Syriac text

[2] *sc* into being

[3] L *than that the Law of God which is set before them be
despised*   it was supposed that the Torah had been offered
to and rejected by the nations of the world outside Israel,
see *E A* , p 105

[4] Or *tortured*

[5] L *they were disobedient and spake against him*

[6] = προσέθεντο , L = προέθεντο (*proposed to themselves*)

[7] Cf viii 58 and Ps xiv 1, liii 1

[8] Or *ignored*

[9] So read by a transposition of two letters.

[10] So Ethiop , but L has *his commandments* (Heb *dābhār* =
word (or commandment), and also *deed*   see *E A* , p 107).

[11] Cf Jer ii 5

The temporary Messianic Kingdom and the End of the World (VII 26–[44])

26 For behold the days come,¹ and it shall be when the signs come which I have foretold to thee, ² and the bride shall be revealed, appearing as a city,² and there shall be revealed she ³ that is now cut off 27 and whoever is delivered from these evils which have been predicted, he shall see my wonders ⁴ 28. For my son the Messiah ⁵ shall be revealed together with those who (are) with him,⁶ and shall rejoice those that remain thirty ⁷ years 29 And it shall be after these years my son the Messiah shall die,⁸ and all those in whom is human breath 30 And the world shall return to its first silence seven days, as it was at the beginning, so that no man is left ⁹

31 And it shall be after seven days that world ¹⁰ shall be awakened,¹¹ which now is not awake, and corruption ¹² shall perish

32. And the earth shall give up those that sleep in

¹ Cf v 1
² L *the bride shall appear, even the city coming forth ,* cf Rev xxi 1 f (the new Jerusalem descending from heaven as a bride), this may have influenced text here, ἡ νῦν μὴ φαινομένη being read ἡ νύμφη κ τ λ See E A , p 114 The Heavenly Jerusalem (= *the city which is now invisible*) is meant
³ *She = ?* the city, true text *the land that is now cut off*, 1 e Paradise, for the juxtaposition cf viii 52, Ap Bar iv , Rev xxii 1 f
⁴ 1 e God's wonders in the Messianic age
⁵ L *my son Jesus* (Christian interpolation)
⁶ 1 e the Messiah's immortal companions, cf vi 26 and note
⁷ L 400, Ar ² 1000, perhaps 30 may have been intended by the Christian editor here to refer to Jesus (see E A , p 115) The temporary Messianic Kingdom is referred to, see E A , p 116
⁸ Death of Messiah nowhere else in Apocalyptic so explicitly referred to, see E A , p 117
⁹ Cf Ap Bar iv 7 ¹⁰ Or *Age* (1 e the future Age)
¹¹ 1 e called into being
¹² The present corruptible world-order vanishes away with the coming of the New Age, cf 1 Cor xv 26

her,[1] and the dust shall give up those that repose therein, and the chambers shall give up the souls that were put in them [2]

33 And the most High shall be revealed upon the throne of judgement . [3]

> [and the end shall come,] [4]
> and compassion pass away,
> and pity be far off,
> and long-suffering be gathered, [5]

34 But my judgement alone shall remain,
> and truth shall stand,
> and faith flourish,

35 And the work [6] shall come,
> and the reward be made known,
> and acts of righteousness [7] shall awake
> and acts of ungodliness shall not sleep.

[36] And the †pit† [8] of torment shall appear,
> but over against this the place of rest,
> the furnace of Gehenna shall be revealed,
> and over against it the Paradise of delights.

[37] And then shall the Most High say to those nations that have been raised [9]
> Gaze and see what [10] ye have denied,

---

[1] Cf Dan xii 2, 1 Thess iv 13, 15, 2 Pet iii 4.

[2] Here apparently the souls of all the dead are spoken of as kept in chambers or "treasuries", elsewhere in the Book only those of the righteous (cf *E A*, p 119 f)

[3] Cf Dan vii 9, Rev xx 11 (one throne, not two as in Rev xx 4)

[4] Cf 1 Cor xv 24, other Versions omit

[5] *i e* ? withdrawn (the attributes of the Divine Judge are referred to).

[6] Or *recompence* (Heb *pĕullā = work* and *reward*)

[7] = acts of charity, cf Ps Sol ix 6, Matt vi 1–4

[8] Reading *gûbā*   text = *bosom*, cf Luke xvi 23, 24. At this point, ver [36] begins the lacuna in the Latin text which was supplied by the *Missing Fragment* discovered by Bensly There was never any lacuna, of course, in the Syriac or other Oriental Versions

[9] From the dead

[10] So Syr text   perhaps *whom* should be read with L and other Versions   For the nations raised for judgement cf Matt xxv 31 f

> or whom ye have not served,
> or whose commandments ye have despised !

[38] Look, therefore, over against you .
> behold here rest and enjoyments,
> and there fire and torment !

Thus shall he speak to them in that Day of Judgement

[39] For the Day of Judgement is thus [1]

[40] on it there is no sun, nor moon, nor stars,
> neither clouds, nor [2] lightning, nor thunder [2],
> neither wind, nor water, nor air [3],
> neither darkness, nor evening, nor morning,

[41] neither summer, nor winter, nor autumn,
> neither heat, nor frost, nor cold,
> neither hail, nor dew, nor rain,

[42] neither noon, nor night, nor day,
> neither light, [nor torch],[4] nor radiance, nor brightness,

save only the splendour of the glory of the Most High from which [5] they [6] are destined to see what hath been ordained [7]

[43] But there shall be an interval as it were a week of years [8] [44] But this is . . . [9] and its law,[10] and to thee only have I made them known.

---

[1] Cf the paraphrase of vers [40]–[42] in Ambrose, *de bono mortis*, xii, and the parallel in *Sibyll Or* iii 89–92, the End = the beginning (see *E A*, p 128 f)

[2] L inverts the order

[3] So L ; perhaps *air* here = thin cloud.

[4] Or *torches* = λαμπάδες (? a gloss)   L omits

[5] *i. e* whereby

[6] L + *all*

[7] Or prepared   the uncreated light of the Divine Presence will reveal what has been prepared for the judgement, cf. Is lx 19 f , Rev xxi 23

[8] Each day = one year.

[9] A word has fallen out, supply *my Judgement* with L. (and so substantially the other Versions).

[10] *i e* prescribed order.

The Debate continued ; Israel's Election and the Problem of Righteousness (VII. [45]—IX. 22)

The Fewness of the Saved (VII [45]-[61])

[45] And I answered and said . O Lord [my Lord],[1] I said even then [2] and say now again, that blessed are all they who have come [3] and have kept the commandments which have been set forth by thee. [46] But concerning those about whom my petition (was made)—who is there, then, of those who have come,[3] who †hath† not sinned [4] ? Or who is there of (those) born who hath not transgressed thy commandment [5] ? [47] And now †It† [6] see that for few shall that coming world effect [7] delight, but for many torment

[48] For there is [8] in us the evil heart
which hath caused us to err from these,[9]
and led us into corruption,
and hath shewn us the ways of death,
and made known to us the paths of perdition,
and removed us far from life ,
and this not of a few, but †perchance† [10] of all who have been [11] !

[49] And he answered and said to me
Hear me, [Ezra],[12] and I will speak to thee,
and once again [13] instruct thee.

---

[1] Omitted by other Versions.
[2] The allusion is to vii 17 f   [3] i e into life
[4] Reading sing , text has *have sinned*   cf viii. 17, Rom x 1
[5] So Ethiop , but L has *covenant* (two readings διαθήκην and διαταγήν)
[6] So read by a slight emendation
[7] Lit *make*
[8] L *hath grown up* (so Ethiop)
[9] Viz commandments, possibly the original text had *God* (see E A , p 132)
[10] Reading *kĕbar* for *ḥebar*
[11] L *who have been created*
[12] So Ar [1], but other Versions omit
[13] Or *anew* or *from the beginning.*

[50] For this cause the Most High hath made not one world but two [1]

[51] Thou, however, because thou hast said there are not many righteous but few   .   [2] hear (the answer) to this   [52] [3] If thou have precious stones and few, against the number of these do thou set lead and clay ! [3]

[53] And I said   How, O Lord, is that possible ?

[54] And he answered and said to me . Not only so, but

ask the earth, and she shall tell thee ;

speak [4] to her, and she shall recount to thee

[55] Say to her · Gold hast thou brought forth, and silver, and copper, [5] and iron, and lead, and clay ; [56] But the silver is more (abundant) than gold, and copper than silver, and iron than copper, and lead than iron, and clay than lead [6]   [57] Do thou, then, reckon up [7] and see, what things are precious and to be desired, [8] [9] the many or the few ? [9]

[58] And I answered and said   O Lord my Lord Things abundant are what are worthless, and things few are precious

[59] And he answered and said to me . Do thou, then, reckon up in thine own mind [10] what thou hast thought !   Because everyone who hath a little that (is) rare rejoiceth over it more than that one who

---

[1] Here the dualism of the Apocalyptic view comes to bold expression

[2] L + *while the ungodly abound*   some words have fallen out in the Syriac

[3] The sentence is really a question , *Wilt thou set with them*, etc , *i e* the number of the elect cannot be increased by the addition of baser elements   The Syriac translator seems not to have understood the verse

[4] L *intreat*   For address to the earth cf viii 2 , Job xvi 18

[5] L *bronze* (*æramentum*)   The list of metals, etc , is interesting, especially in its order

[6] What is rare is precious (notice the emphasis on this).

[7] Lit *make comparison ,* cf iv 31

[8] Lit *dear*

[9] L *that which is abundant or that which is rare,*

[10] Cf. iv 31 and note.

hath what is abundant. [60.] So also is the promise of my judgement, for I rejoice [and delight] [1] over the few who live,[2] because they it is who now strengthen my glory, and for whose sake my name is now extolled [61] And I am not pained over the multitude of those who are perishing, for these are they who now

> are made like a breath,[3]
> and as the smoke [4] are they counted,
> and are comparable unto the flame,
> who are burnt [5] and extinguished

Man's Evil Case bewailed (VII [62]–[74])

[62] And I answered and said: Oh, what hast thou done,[6] O earth, [that these have been born from thee and are going to perdition!] [7] If now the intelligence [8] is from the dust like the rest of creation, [63] it would have been better if also the dust had not been,[9] in order that the intelligence [8] might not (have) come into being [10] from thence.

[64] Now, however, the intelligence [8] groweth with us, and on this account we are tormented, because while we know it we are perishing.

[65] Let the race of men mourn,
>   but the beasts of the field rejoice!
>   let all who are born lament,
>   but the cattle and the flock exult ! [11]

---

[1] Other Versions omit
[2] Other Versions *are saved*
[3] Or *vapour*, cf Ps cxliv 4, James iv 14, *Ap Bar* lxxxii 3
[4] Cf *Ap Bar* lxxxii 6
[5] L + *and burn hotly.* [For the sentiment expressed in the verses cf Wisd. ii 4, and in this Book, xiii 10 f   The Gentiles are referred to, cf *Ap Bar* lxxxii 3 f]
[6] L. *brought forth*
[7] An expansion (cf also Ar [1])   L omits
[8] Or *mind* (= voῦς)   [9] L *been born*
[10] Lit *might not be*   For the sentiment cf iv 12
[11] Lit *delight :* the sentiment expressed would be startling to the ancients.

[66] For it is far better for them than for us, because they do not expect [1] the judgement, neither do they know torture, nor hath life after death been promised to them [67] For what do we profit that we live,[2] but are to suffer torment [3]?

[68.] For all who are born
are defiled with sins,[4]
and are full of iniquities,
and upon them their offences weigh heavily!

[69] And if after death we were not coming into judgement, it had been much better for us!

[70] And he answered and said to me . And when the Most High made [5] the world, [6] and Adam and all that came from him,[6] he first prepared the judgement, and the things which pertain to the judgement.[7]

[71.] And now from thine (own) words understand that thou hast said that the intelligence groweth with us [72] Therefore the inhabitants of the earth are on this account to suffer torment, because while they have intelligence [8] they have committed iniquity, and have received commandments but have not kept them, yea the Law which was bestowed upon them [9] they have rejected [10]

[73] And what is there for them to say in the judgement [11]? Or how shall they [12] open their mouth and speak [12] in the last time? [74] For, how long a time hath the Most High been long-suffering [13] with the inhabitants of the world—and not indeed for their sakes but for the sake of the times ordained?

[1] Or *hope for*
[2] Lit *living we live* (emphatic), *i e* are to live hereafter.
[3] Lit *being tortured suffer torture* (emphatic).
[4] Cf Ecclus xii 14, *Ap Bar* xxi. 19
[5] Lit *making made*
[6] Or *also for Adam and all that came from him*
[7] Note the predestinarian idea, and cf iii 6
[8] Or *mind*
[9] Or *ordained for them*
[10] Or *set at nought* (ἠθέτησαν).
[11] Note the forensic representation (cf vii 37), and see *E A.*, p 140
[12] L *answer.*   [13] Cf iv. 37.

The state of the Soul between Death and Judgement (VII [75]–[101])

[75.] And I answered and said : If I have found favour before thee, O Lord [my Lord],[1] make known to thy servant this also, whether after death now, when we give up, each one of us, our soul—whether we are to be kept in rest until those times come in which thou shalt renew thy creation,[2] or are we to suffer torment forthwith [3] ?

[76.] And he answered and said to me · I will make known to thee concerning this also; but do not thou mingle thyself with the rebellious,[4] nor number thyself with those that suffer torment [77] For thou hast a treasure of works [5] laid up with the Most High, and it shall not be shewn to thee until the last times [6]

[78] But concerning death the teaching [7] is : When the decisive [8] decree of judgement goeth forth from the Most High concerning a man that he shall die,

as the spirit separateth from the body,
that it may be sent [9] to him who gave it,[10]
it first of all worshippeth the glory of God [11]

[79] But if it be of the deniers, or of those who have not kept the ways [12] of the Most High, or of those who have hated the God-fearers [13]— [80.] these souls

---

[1] L omits.
[2] Cf *Ap Bar* xxxii 6 and Gal vi 15, 2 Cor vi 17; Matt. xix 28, 2 Pet iii 13, Rev xxi 1
[3] Lit *from now*
[4] Lit. *those who resist*
[5] Cf viii 36, *Ap Bar* xiv 12, and see *E A*, p. 143
[6] Cf *Ap Bar* xxiv 1
[7] Lit. *the word* or *speech* · L *sermo.*
[8] Lit *end* · L *terminus*
[9] L. *ut dimittatur iterum*
[10] Cf Eccles xii 7
[11] Apparently it remains only temporarily in the Divine Presence at this stage, according to our author, see *E.A.*, p 144
[12] L *the way*   [13] Cf. v. 29.

enter not into the chambers,[1] but henceforth are [2] in torment,[3] sighing and anguished, in seven ways.[4]

[81] The first way   that they have resisted the Law of the Most High   [82] The second way   that they are unable [5] to repent and do good works [5] whereby to live. [83] The third way   that they see the reward laid up for those who have believed [6]   [84] The fourth way   when [7] they know and understand the torment that is prepared for them at the last. [8] [Wherein the souls of the ungodly shall be reproached, because while they had the time for service they did not subject themselves to the commandments of the Most High] [8]   [85] The fifth way   that they see the chambers of the other souls, that are guarded by angels in great quietness   [86] The sixth way: that they see the torment which is made ready for them henceforth [9]

[87] The seventh way, which exceedeth all the ways aforesaid ·

that they pine away through [10] confusion,
and come to an end through shame,[11]
and burn through fear,

in that they see the glory of the Most High before whom [12] they now sin in their life,[12] and before whom they are destined at the last to be judged.

[88] Of those, however, who have kept the way

[1] Or *treasuries*, cf iv 35

[2] I, *wander about* (they have no resting-place)

[3] L + *ever*

[4] *i e* manners or kinds

[5] L *to make a good repentance*

[6] L + *the covenants of the Most High* (so Ethiop Ar [1]), omitted in Syriac (but see next verse)

[7] = ὅτε (for ὅτι)

[8] Added by Syriac   It seems to be a paraphrastic expansion of the words (*the covenants of the Most High*) omitted in the previous verse

[9] *i e* immediately to follow in the intermediate state before the Judgement (the fourth way refers to torments *after* the Judgement), see *E A*, p 146 f

[10] Lit *from*

[11] For the reading of L here cf. *E A.*, p 147.

[12] L. *they have sinned in life.*

of the Most High, this is the way,[1] when [2] the day
cometh that they shall be delivered [2] from this corruptible vessel [3]   [89] For in the time when they
dwelt therein they served the Most High painfully,
and at all hours endured danger, in order perfectly
to keep his Law who had given them the Law [4]

[90] Wherefore this is the word concerning them.

[91] First they behold with great joy the glory
of the Most High, who hath guided [5] them, and they
rest [and come] [6] by seven ways [7]

[92] The first way [8]   because [9] with much toil they
have striven to overcome the evil thought [10] which
was fashioned with them, that they might not go
astray [11] from life to death

[93.] The second way [8] that they see [12] the whirl
whereby the souls of the ungodly are whirled and
driven about,[12] and the torment reserved for them

[94] The third way [8] · that they see the witness
which their fashioner witnesseth concerning them,
because they kept the Law entrusted (to them).

[95] The fourth way [8] . that they [see and] [13]
understand the rest in which they now, as soon as they
have been gathered into their chambers,[14] rest in
profound rest, and are guarded by angels; and the
glory which is reserved for them at the last.

[96.] The fifth way . that they rejoice that [15] they
have fled now from what is corruptible, and that [15]
they inherit what is future, and further they see the
straitness and much toil from which they have been

---

[1] L the order (= ἡ τάξις)   [2] L they shall be separated
[3] Cf 1 Cor xv 53   Notice that the body in our passage
is regarded as the prison-house of the soul.
[4] L the law of the lawgiver   A variant reading in the Syr
is the Law given to them
[5] L receives   [6] L and other Versions omit.
[7] L. orders (so Ethiop)   [8] L order (so Ethiop)
[9] = ὅτι "that"   [10] Cf iii 20
[11] L that it might not lead them astray
[12] R V (= L) the perplexity in which the souls of the ungodly
wander
[13] L omits.   [14] Lit treasuries.
[15] Lit. how = quomodo (= ὡς).

freed, and the wide room [1] which they are destined to receive, and the delights they shall gain, and be immortal.

[97] The sixth way when it shall be shewed to them how their faces are destined to shine as the sun, and how they are destined to be made like the light of the stars,[2] and no more corruptible.

[98] The seventh way [3] which exceedeth all these aforesaid .

> that they exult with boldness,[4]
> and are confident and not ashamed,[5]

and hasten to behold the face of him whom they served in their life and from whom [6] they are destined to be glorified, and from whom they are destined to receive reward [6] [99] These are the ways [7] of the souls of the righteous which from henceforth are announced [8], and the way of tortures aforesaid [9] shall the resisters receive [9]

[10] [Such souls ascend not into chambers,[11] but from henceforth are afflicted with tortures and are grieved and lament in seven ways][10]

[100] And I answered and said . Is then [place or] [12] time given to the souls,[13] after they separate from the body, to see what thou hast told me ?

[101] And he answered and said to me : Seven days have they freedom [14] that in these seven days

---

[1] Lit. *widths* (plural), cf Ps iv 1. The word might be rendered *refreshment*

[2] Based on Dan xii 3, cf Matt xiii 43, *Ap Bar* li 10, 1 Enoch xxxix 7, civ 2, the figure denotes immortality. See *E A*, p 151

[3] Cf ver. 87 above   [4] Cf Wisd. v 1

[5] L + *are glad without fear*

[6] L *they are destined to receive their reward in glory.*

[7] L *this is the order*   [9] = ἐπαγγέλλονται.

[9] L (cf R V) *they that would not give heed shall suffer henceforth ,* Ethiop *the deniers shall suffer.*

[10] An addition by the Syr , apparently a doublet (? added as a gloss here) of ver 80 above None of the other Versions support this

[11] Lit. *treasuries*   [12] Omitted by the other Versions.

[13] Apparently of the righteous only, see *E A* , p 152.

[14] Lit *seven are the days of their freedom.*

they may see these things aforesaid, and after this they shall be gathered into their chambers

No Intercession on the Day of Judgement
(VII. [102]–[115])

[102] And I answered and said   If I have found favour in thy sight, make known to [1] thy servant this [2] also   whether in the Day of Judgement the righteous can intercede for [3] the ungodly, or intreat the Most High for them——

[103] Either fathers [4] in behalf of their sons,[5] or sons [5] in behalf of their fathers,[4] or brothers in behalf of their brothers, or kinsfolk [6] in behalf of their kinsfolk, or friends in behalf of their friends [6]?

[104] And he answered and said to me : Because thou hast found favour before my sight, I will make known to thee concerning this also   The Day of Judgement is a decisive [7] day, and (one) declaring to all the seal of truth [8]   For as now a father sendeth not a son, or a son his father, or a master his slave, or a friend his dearest that in his stead he may be ill,[9] or sleep, or eat or be healed, [105] so also then can none pray on behalf of any on that day, neither shall one lay [10] a burden on any, for all then bear everyone his own righteousness or his iniquity.[11]

[106] And I answered and said . How is it, then, my Lord, (that) we have found [12] that formerly Abraham prayed for the Sodomites,[13] and also Moses

---

[1] L. + me   [2] L omits this
[3] Lit beg off, apologize for, L excusare = παραιτεῖσθαι + accus
[4] Or parents   [5] Or children
[6] L kinsfolk for their nearest, friends for their dearest
[7] Or determinate
[8] i e the seal of the judge which attests the truth and justice of the sentence (Gunkel)
[9] L may understand (reading ἵνα νοῇ for ἵνα νοσῇ)
[10] Possibly " make himself a burden on " is meant
[11] Cf. Ezek xviii 20
[12] sc in Scripture (written)   [13] Cf Gen xviii 23

in the wilderness for the fathers, when they sinned, [1]
[107.] and Joshua the son of Nun after him for
Israel in the days of Achar, [2] [108] and Samuel in
the days of Saul,[3] and David for the ruin [4] of the people, and Solomon for those in [5] the Sanctuary, [109]
and Elijah for those who received the rain,[6] and for
the dead that he might live, [7] [110] And Hezekiah
for the people in the days of Sennacherib,[8] and many
on behalf of many? [111] If, therefore, now,
when corruption is grown up and mischief multiplied,
the righteous have prayed for the ungodly—why,
O Lord, should it not be so then also?

[112] And he answered and said to me   This
world has an end,[9] and the glory of God [10] abideth not
therein continuously, therefore have the strong
prayed for those who have no strength. [113] But
the Day of Judgement is the end of this world and
the beginning of the future world, which dieth not,
wherein

[114]   corruption is passed away,
and impudicity [11] is dissolved,
and infidelity is abolished,
and righteousness is grown up,
and truth [12] hath arisen [13]

[115] So shall none then be able to compassionate
him who is condemned [14] in the Judgement, nor harm
him who is victorious [in the Judgement] [15]

---

[1] Cf Exod xxxii 11
[2] This is the best attested form, cf Josh vii (where
Achan is the form given), see *E A*, p 158
[3] Cf 1 Sam vii 9, xii 23
[4] A V *destruction*, this is a wrong rendering of θραῦσις =
in LXX *plague*; the ref is to 2 Sam xxiv 15 f
[5] Or *those of;* perhaps *those who (should pray) in the
sanctuary*, cf 1 Kings viii 22 f, 30 f
[6] Cf 1 Kings xviii 42   [7] Cf 1 Kings xvii 20 f.
[8] Cf 2 Kings xix 15 f   [9] L *is not the end*
[10] *i e* the Shekinah or Divine Presence, cf *E A*, p 159
[11] = ἀσέλγεια = L (*intemperantia*), Ethiop *weakness* (=
ἀσθένεια).
[12] = *faithfulness*   [13] Cf for whole verse vi 27, 28
[14] Lit *is overcome* (= ἡττήθη) -   [15] Added by Syriac.

The Promises of future Felicity only mock a Sin-stained Race (VII [116]-[131])

[116] And I answered and said : This is my first and last word, that it would have been better for the earth not to have produced Adam,[1] or or (else) when she did produce him that thou hadst instructed [2] him not to sin   [117] For how doth it profit all who have come [3] to live here [4] in affliction, and when they [5] are dead to await torment ?   [118] Oh, what hast thou done, Adam ! For though it was thou that didst sin, yet the evil [6] was not thine alone, but ours also who are from thee !

[119] For what advantage is there that lo ! there is promised to us an immortal time,[7] whereas we have done the works that bring death ? [8]   [120] And that there hath been made known [9] to us an imperishable hope,[10] whereas we miserably are brought to futility ? [11]   [121] And that there chambers of safety and health are kept, whereas we have behaved wickedly ?   [122] And that the glory [12] of the Most High is destined to protect [13] them who have lived chastely, whereas we proceed in wicked ways ?   [123] And that Paradise, whose fruit withereth not,[14] wherein [15] is delight and healing, is manifested, [124] whereas we do not enter in, because we have

[1] Cf iii. 5
[2] = κατηχεῖν (so Ethiop), L *hindered* (= κατέχειν)
[3] = τοῖς πάρουσι, i e all who are here, L *all that are in this present* (*time*).
[4] Syr *hā*   [5] L *we*
[6] So Ethiop, but L (?) *fall* (*casus*)
[7] So L , but Ethiop *the eternal age*
[8] Lit *dead* (or *mortal*) *works* , cf Heb vi 1
[9] So Ethiop , but L *predicted*.
[10] Cf 1 Pet 1 3
[11] Lit *are become vain*
[12] i e the Shekinah
[13] The Shekinah protects the righteous, see *E A* , p 161.
[14] L *endures incorruptible*
[15] i e in the fruit, cf Ezek xlvii 12, Rev xxii 2

served evil places ?[1]   [125] And that the faces of
the holy ones[2] are destined to shine above the stars,[3]
while our faces shall be blacker than darkness ?[4]
[126] For we did not consider in our life (time),
while we were committing iniquity, that we were
destined to suffer after our death

[127.] And he answered and said to me :   This is
the meaning[5] of the struggle which man who is
born wageth[6] upon the earth,   [128] (that)[7] if
he be vanquished he shall suffer what thou[8] hast
said, but if he be victorious he shall receive what
I[9] have said.

[129] Because this is the way of which Moses,
while he was alive, spake to the people, and said
to them   [10] [Behold, I have set before you to-day,
life and death, good and evil,][10] choose you, then,
life that you may live [10] [you and your seed][10]   [130]
And [they resisted and][11] believed[12] him not, nor the
prophets after him, and[13] even me[14] who have spoken
with them   [131] Therefore shall there be no grief
over their perdition, as there is joy over the life[15] of
those who have believed.[12]

---

[1] So L   but *manners* should be read (τρόποις for τόποις),
cf *E A*, p 162
[2] L *such as practised abstinence*
[3] Cf Dan xii 3
[4] Cf *E A*, p 162
[5] Lit *thought* or *intent*, probably originally = *condition*; cf.
E A, p 162 f
[6] Lit *striveth* (*struggleth*)
[7] Probably a letter has fallen out in the Syriac
[8] Or *I* (probably 2nd person is meant, so L)
[9] Or *thou* (probably 1st person is meant, so L), see *E.A*,
p 163
[10] Addition by Syriac from Deut   xxx   15, 19,   L   and
Ethiop omit
[11] Added by Syriac
[12] Or *obeyed*
[13] *i e* nor
[14] The angel speaks as God
[15] L. *salvation*

E

How can the Perdition of so many of His Creatures be reconciled with God's Character ? (VII. [132]—VIII. 62)

Will the Merciful and Compassionate One suffer so many to Perish ? (VII [132]—VIII 3)

[132] And I answered and said to him · I know, Lord, that now the most High is called [1] the "compassionate," because he compassionateth those who have not yet come into the world [2], [133.] and "gracious," because he is gracious to those who turn [3] to his Law, [134] and "long-suffering," because he is long-suffering with us, with [4] those who sin, because we are his works, [4] [135] and "giver," [5] because he is willing to give rather than exact [6], [136] and "of great mercy," because he greatly multiplieth mercies upon them who are now (in existence), and upon those who have passed away, and upon those who are to come—[137] for if he did not multiply his mercies, [7] the world with its inhabitants could not live [8], [138] and the "Giver," [9] because unless in his goodness he gave, [10] so that evil-doers were eased [11] of their iniquities, not even one of ten thousand men [12] could live, [13] [139] and

[1] The epithets applied to God in the following passage (defining the divine attributes) are based upon Exod xxxiv 6–7, possibly a Midrash on this passage lies behind our text, see *E A*, p 164 f

[2] *i e* are not yet born, though God foresees man's sins, He is yet compassionate

[3] Or *return*

[4] L *to sinners as his works*

[5] So Ethiop   L *(munificus) = bountiful*

[6] *i e* perhaps *granteth pardon* rather than *exacteth punishment*, see *E A*, p 167

[7] ? in the intermediate state, see *E A*, p 167

[8] *i e* in the future life

[9] *i e* of merit (to enable them to escape eternal punishment), see *E A*, p 167 f   [10] *sc* merit

[11] Lit *were lightened*

[12] L *the ten thousandth part of mankind.*

[13] In the future life

" judge," [1] for if he did not pardon them who were created by his word, and disregard [2] the multitude of their iniquities, [140] there would only be left of an innumerable multitude very few [3]

VIII. 1 And he answered and said to me   This world [4] hath the Most High made for the sake of many, but that which is to come for the sake of few   2 But I will expound †a parable†,[5] O Ezra : as when [6] thou shalt ask the earth and it shall say to thee [7] what dust it yieldeth more abundantly, that from which cometh the potsherd, or that from which cometh gold , [7] so is the work [8] of this world   3 Many have been created, but few live [9]

Shall God's Creature, so wonderfully fashioned, perish finally ? (VIII 4–19)

4 And I answered and said ·
   O my soul, absorb understanding,
   And, O my heart,[10] drink discernment ! [11]
5 For without thy will thou camest,
   And departest when thou hast not willed [12]
For power [13] hath only been given thee for [14] life for a brief time
6 O Lord, my Lord,[15] if thou wouldst command [16]

---

[1] So L and other versions—an error, ? read forgiving (see E A , p 168)
[2] L blot out   [3] Lit a small few   [4] Or age
[5] So read (transposing two letters) = the other versions, Syr text a word
[6] Lit as
[7] L (R V) that it giveth very much mould whereof earthen vessels are made, and little dust that gold cometh of
[8] L course (actus), both = ἡ πράξις
[9] L shall be saved , cf Matt xxii 14, and in our Book vii 49–61
[10] L omits O my heart
[11] i e abandon all attempts to understand the riddle
[12] Cf Ap Bar xlviii 14 f   [13] L space   [14] Lit in
[15] L O Lord above us (so also viii 45), see E A , p 171
[16] = " if thou wouldst but," " Oh that thou wouldst " (a Hebraism), cf E A , p 171

thy servant I [1] would pray before thee   And do
thou give us [2] the seed and culture of a new heart [3]
whence (may) come fruits, so that everyone that is
corruptible may be able to live who is clothed with
the form [4] of man   7 For one art thou, and one
fashioning are we, the work of thine hands, as thou
hast said [5] 8 And [6] thou dost indeed quicken [7]
for us now in the womb the body which thou hast
fashioned, and composest the members,   and thy
creature is kept in fire and water,[8] and nine months
doth thy fashioning [9] bear the creature which thou
hast created in it [10]   9 But that which keepeth,
and that which is kept, are both kept by thy keeping
And when the womb giveth again what has been [11]
therein, 10 thou hast commanded that out of the
members [12] should come milk, the fruit of the [full] [13]
breasts, 11 that what hath been fashioned may grow [14]
for a short time   12 And afterwards—

> thou guidest it in thy mercy,
> and nourishest it in thy righteousness,
> and disciplinest it in thy law,
> And admonishest it in thy wisdom—

13 and thou killest it as thy creature,
> and quickenest it as thy work [15]

14 If, then, thou [16] suddenly and quickly [16] destroy-
est this one who hath been fashioned with all this

---

[1] L *we*
[2] = " Ó that thou wouldest give us "
[3] R V *seed unto our heart and culture to our understanding,*
cf Rom xii 2, Ephes iv 23
[4] L *place* (τόπον for τύπον)
[5] Cf Is xlv 11, lx 21, lxiv 8 f   God is one, unique,
Father, and Creator, cf vi 1–6
[6] L + *when*   [7] Lit *quickening quicken*
[8] Man's living organism is compounded of the primal
elements (an Oriental doctrine), cf iv 10, 2 Enoch xxx 15,
with Charles's note
[9] *i e* the womb   [10] L *which is created in it*
[11] L + *created*
[12] L + *that is out of the breasts* (? a gloss)
[13] Added by Syriac   [14] Or *be nourished*
[15] Cf 1 Sam ii 6
[16] L *with a light word* (or *command*)

great labour, according to thy command, for what
purpose, then, came he into being?   15 [1] Now also
I have spoken concerning all men, but even more,
thou knowest, that [1]
  16 concerning thy people I suffer,
      and concerning thine heritage [2]—that concern-
        ing it I mourn,
      and concerning Israel—that concerning him
        I am grieved,
      and concerning Jacob's seed [3]—that concerning
        it I am moved
  17 Therefore behold I will begin to pray and
supplicate before thee for myself and for them,
because lo ! I see the trespasses of us who inhabit
the world,[4] 18 but also now have heard the decree
of judgement [5] that is to come   19 Therefore
      hear my voice,
      and listen to [6] the words of my prayer,[6]
      and I will speak before thee, [O Lord my God] [7]

The Seer's Prayer for the Divine Compassion
on His People, and the Reply (VIII 20–40)

  20 [8] *The beginning of the words of the Prayer of
Ezra which he prayed before he was taken up* [8]
      O Lord that dwellest for ever,[9]
      [10] whose heights are exalted,[10]
      and whose chambers[11] are in the air,

[1] L *But now I will say   Concerning man in general thou
knowest best , but* (Syriac constructs sentence differently).
  [2] Cf Ps xxviii 9   [3] Cf iii 19
  [4] L *that dwell in the land*   [5] Cf v 34
  [6] L *my words* (cf Ethiop)
  [7] Added by Syriac, other versions omit
  [8] This superscription has been inserted into the text by
the Latin, Syriac, and Ethiopic   The piece seems to have
been excerpted early for liturgical purposes, see *E A* , p 175 f
  [9] Cf Is lvii 15
  [10] L *whose are the highest heavens ,* cf Deut x 14
  [11] ? the heavenly Paradise (for phraseology cf Ps civ 3)

21. whose throne is infinite,[1]
    and whose glory is inconceivable, [2]
    before whom the hosts [3] stand in fear,
    at whose word they change to fire and wind,[4]

22. whose word is trustworthy,
    and whose speech abideth, [5]
    whose commandment is strong,
    and whose utterances [6] are terrible,

23 whose look drieth up the deep,[7]
    and whose rebuke [8] melteth the mountains,
    and whose truth beareth witness—[9]

24 .Hear the voice of thy servant,
    and listen to thy creature's petition,
    and regard my words !

25. For while I live I will speak,
    and while I have understanding will I answer.

26. O regard not the trespasses of thy people,
    but them that have served thee in truth,

27 and regard not [10] the follies of the intrigues
    of the ungodly,[10]
    but them that have kept thy covenants in
    ignominy, [11]

28. think not upon those that have behaved them-
    selves badly [12] before thee,
    but remember them that with good will have
    recognized thy fear ! [13]

---

[1] L *inestimable*, the mystery of God's throne is the subject of Ezek 1

[2] Cf Rom xi 33   [3] i e of heaven

[4] Cf. Ps civ 4 (this passage implies the rendering *who maketh his angels winds*, etc, see *E A* , p 178)

[5] = *is constant* (an allusion to the Synagogue prayer *'ĕmeth wĕ-yassîb*, cf *E A* , p 179)

[6] Other versions have singular

[7] The other versions have the plural   [8] = ἀπειλή

[9] So all the versions except Ar [2], which has right reading *remaineth for ever* (see *E A* , p 179), the verse is cited in Greek in *Const Apost* viii 7

[10] L and other versions *the deeds of the ungodly*

[11] L *in tortures ;* the martyrs are meant

[12] L *walked feignedly* (= ? hypocritical adherents of the Law)

[13] i e *fear of thee* = religion, piety, cf Ps xix 10

29. and will not to destroy those that have become
like the cattle,[1]

but regard them that have received [2] the
splendour of [3] thy Law,

30. and be not angry against those who have behaved worse than the beasts,[4]

but love them that have always put their trust
in thy glory

31 Because we and [5]those before us[5] have [6]practised
works of corruption, and behaved madly [6], but thou
because of us sinners art called the Compassionate.
32. For if us, who have no works,[7] thou art
willing to compassionate, thou shalt be named
Gracious One   33. For the righteous who have [8] works
laid up with thee can receive out of their own
works [9]

34 For—

what is man that thou shouldest be (so) angry
with him,

or a corruptible race that thou shouldest be (so)
hot [10] against it ?

35. For in truth

there is none of those born that hath not dealt
wickedly,

Nor of these who exist that hath not sinned !

36 For in this, O Lord [my Lord],[11] shall thy [12]
goodness be known if thou art compassionate towards
them that have no wealth [13] of works.

---

[1] *i e* probably Jews who lived like heathen (? the *'am
hā-āreṣ*)

[2] Due to a misreading of διδάξαντες, L *taught*

[3] L *in splendour*

[4] A more infamous class still (? Jewish informers)

[5] *v l our fathers*

[6] R V *have passed our lives in ways that bring death ,* for
text cf *E A* , p 182

[7] L *+ of righteousness*

[8] L *+ many*

[9] Cf *Ap Bar* xiv 12

[10] *v l bitter*, cf Job vii 17 f (Ps viii 4)

[11] Omitted by other Versions

[12] L. *+ righteousness and*.   [13] Or *power*

The Divine Reply

37 And he answered and said to me   Some things thou hast spoken aright and according to thy words,[1] so shall it be   38 Because in truth I take no thought about the fashioning of the evil doers, or about their death,[2] or about their judgement, or about their perdition, [3] 39 but I delight (rather) over [the coming of] [4] the fashioning of the righteous, and over their life, and over the recompence of their reward   40. For as thou hast said so shall it be.

Mankind is like Seed sown (VIII 41–45)

41 For as the husbandman [who] [5] soweth many seeds [6] and planteth many plants, but not all the seeds live in due season,[7] nor indeed do all the plants strike root, so also they who have [8] come into [8] the world do not all live

42 And I answered and said : If I have found favour in thy sight I would speak [before thee] [9]

43 [10] For the husbandman's seed, if it receive not thy rain, at its (proper) time, will it live ?   Yea rather from much rain it is destroyed [10]

44 But man who hath been fashioned by thine

---

[1] The seer had prayed (ver. 28 f) that God would fix His attention rather on the deeds of the righteous than on those of the ungodly , this part of the petition shall be granted The angel is still the speaker (note the bitter irony)

[2] i e their physical death

[3] i e final perdition

[4] The text of this passage is out of order , perhaps *the coming of* corresponds to *pilgrimage* in L and should follow *righteous* (R V *their pilgrimage   and the salvation, and the reward*) See *E A* , p 185 f

[5] Omit

[6] L + *upon the ground*

[7] Lit *in time*

[8] L *are sown in*

[9] Added by Syriac

[10] The Latin text here is corrupt , as corrected and restored it may be rendered . *Forasmuch as the husbandman's seed, if it come not up, seeing that it hath not received thy rain in due season, or if it be corrupted through too much rain, so perisheth* (R V) See *E A* , p 187

own hands and [1] is made like thine own image,[1]
for whose sake thou hast created all—hast thou
likened him to the seed of the husbandman ? [2]

45 No ! [I beseech thee,] [3] O Lord my Lord,[4]
   spare thy people,
   and compassionate thine heritage——
   thy creature—for thine he is—thou dost compassionate !

The Final Reply ; Let the Seer contemplate the Lot of the Blessed which he is destined to share (VIII. 46–62)

46. And he answered and said to me .
    [5] Things of the present are for them of the pre-
    sent,
    And things of the future are for them who are
    future ! [5]

47. For thou comest far short of being able to
love my creation more than I.[6]

Thou, however, hast many times likened thyself
to the ungodly It must not be so ! 48. But in
this also thou shalt be honoured before the Most
High, 49 because thou hast humbled thyself, as
befitteth thee, and hast not compared thyself [7]
with the righteous Therefore thou shalt be the
more honoured 50. Because with much affliction
shall the inhabitants of the world be afflicted at the
last on account of the great pride [8] that they have
displayed [9]

---

[1] L *is called thine own image because he is made like (unto
thee)* , the Syriac is probably right here

[2] Probably to be taken as a question The seer protests
against the comparison of mankind to seed , contrast the
parable of the Sower in the Gospels

[3] Added by Syr (cf Ethiop)   [4] L *O Lord above us*

[5] For the form of sentence cf vii 25

[6] Cf v 32   [7] L *hast not judged thyself (to be)*

[8] Note the remarkable emphasis on the sin of pride and
the virtue of humility

[9] Lit *with which they have behaved proudly.*

51. But do thou (rather) consider thine own self, and ask concerning the glories of those who are like thyself [1]

52. For for you
is opened Paradise,[2]
and planted the Tree of life; [3]
and the future world [4] prepared,
and delight [5] made ready;
and a City [6] builded,
and a Rest [7] ordained,
and good perfected,[8]
and wisdom completed, [9]

53 And the (evil) root [10] is sealed up from you,
and infirmity from you extinguished,[11]
and Death is hidden,[12]
and Sheol fled; [13]
and corruption is forgotten,
and pains departed from you,

54 And in the consummation the treasures of life
are manifested

55. Do not thou, therefore, again ask any more concerning the many who perish; 56 because they have received liberty and

---

[1] i e probably the righteous dead who already enjoy a foretaste of future felicity

[2] i e the heavenly Paradise which will be reopened after the last Judgement for the righteous

[3] In Paradise, cf vii 133, Rev ii 7, and see E A, p 191.

[4] Or age, for the idea cf E A, p 191

[5] L plenteousness

[6] i e the heavenly Jerusalem

[7] i e the rest in heaven, cf Heb iii 18 f

[8] Cf Ephes ii. 10

[9] L being perfect aforehand (R V) Cf 1 Cor ii 7

[10] Cf iii 22, 1 Enoch xci 8 (root a technical term in these connections)

[11] The sources of sin in man will have been removed in the future Age

[12] Death, of course, will be abolished, cf Is xxv 8, Rev xxi 4

[13] Cf Ap Bar xxi 23 (the underworld is personified, as in Rev vi 8)

they have despised the Most High,
his Law also they have scorned much,
and have made his ways to cease :[1]

57. Yea, his saints they have trampled upon,[2] and
58 they have said in their heart that there is no God,[3]
while they verily [4] know that they shall surely [5] die.

59 Therefore as these things aforesaid await
you, so also †thirst and† [6] torment (are) destined
for them   For the Most High willed not that men
should perish, 60 but these who have been created
dishonoured the name of their Maker and were un-
grateful [and confessed me not—] [7] who [8] have prepared life for them   61 Therefore my Judgement
hath drawn nigh, 62 which (thing) I have not made
known to the many, but (only) to thee and to the few
like thee.[9]

The Signs of the End reviewed (VIII 63—IX 12)

63 And I answered and said · Behold now
(already), O Lord, thou hast made known to me the
great number of the signs that thou art about to
do in the last days, but thou hast not made known
to me at what time [10]

IX 1 And he answered and said to me · Measure
carefully in thy mind,[11] †and† [12] when thou seest that
a part of the signs aforesaid is past, 2 then understand
that it is the time wherein the Most High is about to
visit [13] the world made by him.   3. And when there
shall appear in the world

---

[1] L Ethiop *have forsaken* (*his ways*)
[2] Cf v 29   [3] Cf vii 23, Ps xiv 1
[4] Lit *knowing*   [5] Lit *dying*
[6] So read by a slight emendation, Syriac text has (*the
torment that is prepared*) *is thirsty;* cf for the representation,
Luke xvi 24
[7] Omitted by L   [8] L *to him who* (*had*)
[9] *i e* to the seers and apocalyptists like Salathiel-Ezra
[10] Contrast Acts 1 7
[11] Lit *thyself*   [12] So read, Syr text *that*
[13] Cf vi 18

>   quakings of places,[1]
>   and tumult of assemblages,[2]
>   and schemings of peoples,
>   and commotion of leaders,
>   and confusion of princes—

4 then perceive that it is of these (things) the
Most High hath spoken formerly   5 For as with
respect to everything in the world, its beginning is
known [3] and its end manifest, 6   so also (are) the
times of the Most High   their beginnings are known
in portents, [and signs] [4] and powers,[5] and their end
in requital [6] and signs.   7. And it shall be (that)
everyone that shall survive,[7] and everyone   that
shall be able to flee [8] through his works or through
his faith whereby he hath believed—   8   he shall be
left (safe) from the peril aforesaid, and shall see my
salvation [9] in my land and in my borders [10] which I
have sanctified for myself eternally [11]   9 And then
shall they be amazed who have now neglected [12]
my ways, and they shall be in torments who have
despised and abandoned them [13]   10 For all who
did not recognize me in their life (time), when I was
dealing bountifully with them, and all who have
treated my Law with contempt,[14] those [15] (viz) who

[1] i e earthquakes (cf v 8), others stir (i e excitement)
of places
[2] L of peoples
[3] L defective, the text here may originally have been
obscure (ἀφανής corrupted to ἐμφανής), cf E A , p 202
[4] L omits   [5] Or mighty works
[6] L Ethiop in effects.   [7] Cf vi 25, vii 28
[8] i e escape
[9] i e the Messianic salvation, cf vi 25
[10] Cf xiii 35
[11] Lit from eternity   the specially sacred character of the
Holy Land is often insisted on in late Jewish literature, cf
ix 8, xii 34, xiii 48 f , Ap Bar xxix 2.
[12] L abused
[13] i e my ways, another reading in L makes them refer
to torments
[14] Lit behaved themselves proudly against
[15] So Syriac, but this may be an error of the translator who
misread ὡς as οἷς, other Versions while = ὡς

had liberty,   12 and while the place of long-suffering [1] was (still) open to them, did not heed, but scorned— for these it is necessary that after death they should know [2]

The Fewness of the Saved further justified
(IX 13–22)

13 Do thou, therefore, not search out [3] henceforth [4] how the ungodly shall be tormented, but inquire how the righteous shall live [5]—they whose is the world, and for whom also the world hath come into existence [6] 14 And I answered and said   15 [7] Now also again I say, and hereafter will say again, that more are those who perish than those who live [8]   16 just as the waves are more than the small drop [9]

17 And he answered and said to me
    As the place,[10] so also (are) its seeds,[11]
    and as the flowers, so also (are) the colours,[12]
    and as the work, so also (are) the odours,[13]
    and as the husbandman, so also (is) the threshing floor [14],

18 for there was in the time of the world [15] when I had prepared for those who now are, before they were

---

[1] So Ethiop, but L and Ar 1 *repentance*, cf (for latter) Wisd xii 10, Heb xii 17
[2] So Ethiop, but L and Ar 1 + *by* (or *in*) *torment*
[3] L *be curious*   [4] L *any longer*
[5] So Ethiop, but L and Ar 1 *be saved*
[6] Cf for the whole verse *Ap Bar* xlviii 48 f
[7] L prefixes to this *I have already said*
[8] L *be saved*, cf vii 47
[9] Cf iv 48 f   [10] L *field*
[11] Or *sowings*, i e good ground produces good crops
[12] i e the finest flowers produce the most brilliant colourings
[13] L *creation* (= κτίσις), but Ethiop Ar 1 *judgement* (= κρίσις), adopted by R V, and this probably equals the true text of Syriac   See further *E A*, p 207
[14] Or *harvest*
[15] = ἐν καιρῷ αἰῶνος, i e *in the time of eternity*   For the meaning cf *E A*, p 207

(in existence) a world for them to live in, and no man withstood me—for indeed there was none (in existence).

19 And now that they have been created upon the world that standeth firm,[1] and upon a table that lacketh not, and upon a Law [2] that is unsearchable, they are become corrupt in their deeds,[3]

and I regarded my world, and lo ! it was lost !
and my cosmos,[4] and lo ! it was in peril—
on account of the manners [5] of its inhabitants

21 And I saw and spared a small few,[6] and saved me a grape out of a cluster, and a plant out of a great forest.

22 Let the multitude, therefore, perish because it hath come into being in vain, but let my grape be preserved, and my plant, which have been produced [7] with much toil

Conclusion of the Vision (IX 23–25)

23. But if thou wilt separate thyself [8] seven more days—but thou shalt not [again] [9] fast therein, 24 and go thou to a field of flowers, where no house hath been built, and eat thou of the flowers of the field only, and flesh thou shalt not taste, nor shalt thou drink wine,[10] but flowers only, 25 and petition the Most High zealously,[11] and I will come unto thee and speak with thee

---

[1] Or *is made ready* (the text should run [cf L] *a world prepared with a table that faileth not, and an unexplorable pasture*, in reference to Paradise, see *E A* , p 207 f)

[2] *νόμος = Law* confused with *νομός = pasture*

[3] L *manners*

[4] A synonym for *world* is used = *tĕbhēl*

[5] Or possibly *perversions*   L *devices*

[6] Lit *a small little*   L *vix valde, but not greatly* (R V)

[7] L *I have produced*

[8] L *cease*

[9] Added by Syriac

[10] Cf 2 Macc v 27

[11] L *continually*

VISION IV
(IX. 26—X 59)

Introduction (IX. 26–28)

26 And I went, as he commanded me, into the field which is called Arpad,[1] and sat there by [2] the flowers of the land, and did eat of the herbs [3] of the pasture, and the eating thereof was to my satisfaction   27 And it came to pass after seven days, as I lay upon the grass, that my heart again began to be moved [4] [upon me] [5] as before,   28 and my mouth was opened, and I began to speak before the Most High.

The Glory of the Law and Israel : a Contrast
(IX. 29–37)

29 And I said   O Lord [my Lord,] [6] thou didst verily reveal thyself [7] to our fathers in the wilderness [of Sinai] [8] when they went forth out of Egypt, and when they went through the wilderness, [9] through a land wherein was no fruit, and through which no man hath passed [9], 30. and thou didst say [to them] [10]

[1] So Ethiop (cf 2 Kings xviii 34), L (best reading) *Ardat*   a symbolical name of a mysterious place (? Arcadia), see *E A* , p 212 f
[2] L *in* or *among*   [3] Lit *roots*   [4] Or *troubled*
[5] Omitted by L , cf Ps xlii 5 (" disquieted *upon* me ") · cf vi 36
[6] So Ethiop , but L omits   [7] L + *among us*
[8] Omitted by other Versions
[9] L. *the untrodden and unfruitful*   cf Jer ii 6 [in the last clause of ver 29 there is a scribal error in the Syriac text, read *wĕlâ* instead of *wĕkad*]
[10] So Ar [2] and Arm , other Versions omit.

Do thou, Israel, hear me,
and, seed of Jacob, listen to my words ! [1]

31 For, behold, I sow in you my Law, and it shall produce in you fruits [of righteousness],[2] and ye shall be glorified in it for ever

32 [3] But our fathers received the Law, and kept it not,
and commandments, and did not perform them [3]

[4] And they had the fruits of the Law which perish not, for they could not perish because it is thine [4]

33 Those, however, who received it perished, because they kept not what had been sown in them

34. And this is the rule that when the earth receiveth seed, or the sea a ship, or any other vessel [what hath been put therein] [5] (viz) the food, [6] [7] or what hath been put, or what hath been kept [7]—

35 these [8] are destroyed, but these that received them [9] remain But with us it hath not been so;

36. but we who have received the Law and sin perish together with our heart [10] which accepted it   37 Thy Law, however, perisheth not, but abideth in its glory.[11]

The Vision of the Disconsolate Woman
(IX. 38—X 24)

38. And while I spake these things in my heart,[12] I lifted up mine eyes and beheld a woman on the

[1] Cf Ps l 7   [2] Omitted by other Versions
[3] Note the parallelism of the two lines, this is lost in L
[4] *And the fruit of the law did not perish, neither could it, for it was thine* (R V = L)
[5] ? repeated from next clause accidentally (see *E A*, p 217)
[6] L + *or drink* (so other Versions, but Ethiop doubtful)
[7] L [*and when it cometh to pass that that which is sown*], *or that which is launched, or the things which have been received* [*come to an end*], R V (bracketed clauses not in Syriac)
[8] i e the things put in   [9] i e the receptacles
[10] Which is evil and perishable
[11] Cf Rom vii 14, 2 Cor iii 7 f , and for the whole passage *Ap Bar* xiv 19
[12] i e according to the Hebrew idiom " thought these things "

right side,[1] mourning and weeping with a loud voice, while she [2] sighed in her soul [2] [and was greatly distressed],[3] and her clothes were rent, and dust was cast upon her head. 39 And I dismissed the thoughts which I was debating,[4] and turned to her and said to her . 40 Why dost thou weep, and art distressed in thy soul ? 41 And she answered and said to me   Suffer me, my lord, to weep unchecked [5] and continue further to sigh, because my soul is greatly embittered and I am much humbled [6]

42 And I said to her   Tell me what hath befallen thee   43 And she answered and said to me   I, thine handmaid, was barren, and did not bear, though I was with my husband thirty years   44 And I every day and every hour, during these thirty years, was petitioning and supplicating the Most High by day and by night. 45 And it came to pass after [these] [7] thirty years

God heard [the voice of] [8] thine handmaid,
and saw her humiliation [9],
and looked upon my distress,
and gave me a son

And I rejoiced and delighted in him greatly, I and my husband and all my fellow townsfolk,[10] and we glorified [11] the Mighty One [12], 46 and I reared him with very great toil   47 And when he was grown up I came to take him a wife, and I made a day of feasting [and much merriment] [13]

X 1 And it came to pass that when my son entered into his wedding-chamber he fell down and

---

[1] Cf iv 47
[2] L *was much grieved in mind*
[3] Omitted in L
[4] Lit *cogitating*
[5] Lit *upon myself*
[6] Or *afflicted*
[7] Omitted by other Versions
[8] This is probably the true text, though it is omitted by the other Versions
[9] Barrenness was a reproach, cf Luke i 25
[10] Lit *all the sons of my town*
[11] It was a religious duty to " give God the glory ", cf Luke xvii 18
[12] *i e.* the Almighty, cf vi 32, x 24, xi 43, xii 47
[13] Added by Syriac, cf Matt xxii 2

F

died.   2 But I overturned the lights,[1] and all my
fellow-townsmen [2] rose up to console me ; and I
remained quiet until the next day and until the
night.[3]   3   [4] And after they were all asleep and believed that I also was asleep,[4] then I arose by night,
and fled and came as, [behold],[5] thou seest to this
field   4 And I am resolved that I will not again
enter the city, but that here I will be, and will
neither eat nor drink, but will continually mourn and
fast till I die

5 And I dismissed [6] my thoughts which I had
been debating,[7] and I answered in anger and said
to her ·   6 [8] Thou art more foolish, woman, than all
women ! [8]   Seest thou not our grief and what hath
befallen us ?   7 that [lo !] [9] Sion, the mother of us [10]
all, is in great affliction, and humiliated with great
humiliation ? 8 But it is right now to mourn—
[11] we all mourn , for thou indeed art grieved on
account of one son, [but we—the whole world—on
account of our mother] [12]   9 But ask the earth, and
she shall tell thee , because [13] she is bound to mourn
. . . ,[14] because many are they who have come into
being [15] upon her,   10 and from the beginning all
who have come into being [15] upon her, and the others
who (are to) come, lo ! they [16] all go to perdition, and
their multitude is for destruction   11. Who then
ought to mourn the more, she who hath lost all this
multitude, or thou who mournest for one ?

12 But if thou sayest to me : My mourning is not

[1] Cf Matt xxv 7   [2] See note [10], ix 45
[3] i e until the night of the next day
[4] R V *And it came to pass when they had all left off to comfort
me to the end I might be quiet* (see E A , p 221)
[5] Added by Syriac
[6] Lit *left*   [7] Lit *cogitating*
[8] *Thou foolish woman above all other* (R V = L)
[9] Added by Syriac   [10] Cf Gal iv 26
[11] L + *seeing that*   [12] Added by Syriac.
[13] L (rightly) *that* (=ὅτι also *because*)
[14] There is clearly a lacuna in the sense , Syriac omitted
some words, L + *the fall of so many*
[15] Lit *have been*   [16] L + *almost (pene)*

like the earth's, because I have lost the fruit of my
womb
> which I bare with pains,
> and reared [1] with sorrows—

13 the earth, however, according to the nature of
the earth [2]   the multitude that came upon it is gone
as it came   14 then [3] I will again say to thee . Just
as thou hast borne with travail, so also the earth hath
given her fruit from (the) beginning, man, to him
who made her [4]   15 Now, therefore,
> keep thy pain to thyself, [5]
> and bear bravely [6] the evil that hath befallen thee !

16. For if thou wilt acknowledge as just [7] the
decree of judgement of the Most High, thou shalt
(again) receive thy son in (due) time, [8] and shalt be
praised among women.   17 Go, therefore, into the
city unto thy husband

18 And she answered and said to me . I will not
do so, nor will I go into the city, nor unto my husband,
but here will I die !

19 And I continued further to speak with her, and
I said to her   20 No, woman ! No, woman ! Do
not do this thing, but
20 be convinced of [9] Sion's misfortune,
> and be consoled because of Jerusalem's sorrow !
21 For [behold !] [10] thou hast seen
> our sanctuaries [11] laid waste, [12]

---

[1] L brought forth
[2] i e as regards the earth, such (dying) is according to the
course of nature (see E A , p 224)   [3] Lit and
[4] i e man, earth's highest product, produced with so
much pains, is constantly being gathered in (by death) by the
Creator   This seems to be the meaning, cf E A , p 224
[5] Lit within thyself   [6] With strength
[7] Cf Ps Sol , viii 7, 11 16, Luke vii 29, 35 (an act of piety)
[8] i e either by the son's restoration to life, or by having
another son
[9] Or prevailed on by   [10] Added by Syriac
[11] Other Versions have the singular
[12] Syriac text that they are laid waste (in the same way
prefixing that before each of the verbs throughout the following
clauses), cf 1 Macc 1 39

and our altars [1] overthrown,
and our Temple demolished,
[2] and our service abolished [2],
22 and our song taken away, [3]
and our glorying [4] ceased, [5]
and the light of our lamp quenched,[6]
and the ark of the covenant carried off, [7]
and our saints [8] defiled,
and the name that is called upon us [9] polluted,
and our nobles [10] dishonoured,
and our priests burnt in the fire,[11]
and our Levites taken captive,
and our virgins are defiled,
and our wives forcibly dishonoured,
[12] and our seers seized,
and our watchmen scattered [12],
and our youths enslaved,
and our heroes made weak
23 and what exceedeth all—with regard to Sion's seal,[13]

[1] L *altar*
[2] L *our psaltery is brought low* (cf Ethiop) *psaltery* or *harp* a symbol of Temple service, Syriac interprets, cf E A , p 226
[3] L *is silenced*
[4] Or ? *hymning*, or *our pride*, i e the sacrificial service.
[5] Lit *fallen*
[6] This marked the cessation of the sacrificial service, cf 1 Macc iv 50, and see E A , p 226
[7] This really occurred at the destruction of the first Temple, for its meaning here cf E A , p 226 f
[8] L *holy things* = the holy vessels
[9] i e the divinely bestowed name of Israel, cf Gen xxxii 28
[10] i e the ruling classes
[11] Cf Josephus, *War*, VI 5 1 (two priests threw themselves into the fire " and were burnt together with the holy house ")
[12] L *our righteous men carried away, our little ones betrayed*, possibly the Syriac should be emended so as to read *our pious ones are seized, our righteous scattered* . see further E A , p 228
[13] i e ? Sion's independence—possibly there is a reference to the issue of a national coinage in A D 66–70, cf E A , p. 229 f

the seal of her glory hath been taken away now,
and given up into the hand of them that hate
us !

24 Do thou, then, shake off from thyself [1] the
multitude of thy sorrows,
so that the Mighty One may be reconciled [2] to
thee,
and the Most High may give thee rest [3] from the
sorrows of thy toil ! [3]

Sion's Glory ; the Vision of the Heavenly Jerusalem (X 25–28)

25 And it came to pass, while I was talking with
her, [and] [4] lo ! her countenance shone exceedingly,
and as the appearance of lightning became the look of
her face [5] And I feared greatly [to approach unto
her, and my heart was much amazed] [6] And while I
was cogitating what this [vision] [7] might be, 26. suddenly she cried with a loud and fearful voice, so that
the whole earth was moved at her voice [8] 27 And
I saw, and lo ! the woman was no longer visible to
me, but a City that was builded,[9] and a place became
visible as of great foundations [10] And I was afraid
and cried with a loud voice and said, 28. Where is
the angel Uriel who from the first day [11] came unto

[1] L + *thy great heaviness and put away* (the words were
accidentally omitted by the Syriac translator), see *E A* ,
p 230
[2] Or *propitious*
[3] L *even ease from thy travails* (R V)
[4] Omit   [5] Cf Luke ix 29
[6] So Ar [1], the clause has been omitted (accidentally) by
the Latin translator
[7] L and Ethiop omit.
[8] Cf Gen xxvii 34
[9] *i e* already built, so all the Oriental Versions, but L.
was being built (cf ver 42, R V)
[10] Cf Rev xxi 19 f
[11] L *from the first* (so Ethiop. Ar [1]), cf. iv 1 for the first
appearance of Uriel.

me ?   Because he (it is) who hath caused me to come
into the multitude of this agitation,[1]
        and mine end [2] is made corruption,[3]
        and my prayer ignominy.

The Vision interpreted (X. 29–57)

29 And while I was speaking these things, [lying
on the ground as though dead],[4] the angel came unto
me who had come unto me formerly [5], and he saw
me 30 lying on the ground as though dead,[6] and
my understanding was confused, and he took me by
my right hand and strengthened [7] me, and set me
upon my feet,[8] and said to me :
   31 What aileth thee,
          And why art thou disquieted ?
        And wherefore is thy mind confused,
          and the understanding of thy heart ?
32 And I said to him   Because thou hast forsaken
me ! For I did as thou badest me (and) also (went
out) [9] into the field, and lo ! I have seen—and see [10]
—that which I am unable to explain.[11]

33 And he answered and said to me   Stand [12] upon
thy feet,[12] and I will make known to [13] thee.

34 And I said to him   Speak on, my Lord, and
only do not forsake me lest I die [14] before my time [14]

---

[1] Cf *Shepherd of Hermas*, Vis I ii 1, Vis III 1 5
[2] So all the Versions, perhaps the Hebrew text was corrupt
and the word *prayer* stood originally here (*těfillāthî* corrupted
to *taklîthî = my end*)
[3] Here also a Hebrew corruption may be suspected, *lěhebel*
= " into vanity," having been misread *lěhebel*
[4] Added by Syriac (? from next clause)
[5] Or *at first*
[6] Cf Dan viii 17 f, x 9 f, 15, Rev i 17
[7] Cf Dan x 18   [8] Cf v 15, vi 13, 17
[9] Probably a word has fallen out of the Syriac text here
[10] The vision is still present to his mind's eye.
[11] L *to express ;* cf 2 Cor xii 4.
[12] Cf v 15, vi 13, 17, x 30   L and other versions *like a
man*
[13] L. *advise.*   [14] Ethiop. *suddenly :* L. *to no purpose.*

35 Because I have seen what I do not. understand, [1]
and hear what I am incompetent (to grasp) [2]
36 Or is it that my understanding deceiveth me,[3]
and my soul [4] beholdeth a dream [4] ?
37 But now I beseech thee, my Lord, make known
to thy servant concerning this fearful vision [5]
38. And he answered and said to me .
   Hear me and I will teach thee,
   and reveal [6] to thee concerning the things thou
      art afraid of [7],
because the Most High hath revealed to thee many
secrets.
39 For he hath seen thy right conduct,
   how [8] thou grievest much [9] for thy people,
   [and mournest much for thy people,] [10]
   and mournest much for Sion
40 This, then, is the matter [11]   41. The woman who
appeared to thee a little while ago, who was mourning
and whom thou didst begin to console,   42. and now
[12] she appeareth not as a woman to thee,[12] but hath
appeared to thee as a City that is being built [13]
43 and whereas [14] she told thee of the misfortune of
her son—this is the explanation   44 This woman
whom thou hast seen, this is Sion which thou now
seest [15] as a City being built [13]   45 And whereas [14]
she said to thee concerning herself that she had been
barren thirty years—(it is) because [16] she was in the
world [16] three thousand [17] years when no offering was

---

[1] Or *have not understood* (*known*).
[2] Lit (*what*) *I am unversed* (or *unskilful*) *in*
[3] L *is deceived*   [4] L *dreameth*   [5] L *this perplexity.*
[6] L *tell*   [7] Cf v 32, vii 49   [8] Lit *that*
[9] So Ethiop , L *continually*
[10] Accidental repetition in the Syriac text
[11] = οὗτός ἐστιν ὁ λόγος, " the matter is as follows "
[12] L *thou seest the likeness of the woman no more*
[13] Cf L (*in building*) the participle is used in Syr = οἰκοδο-
μουμένη   [14] Lit *that*
[15] In vision. The woman = Sion, i e the heavenly Jerusalem (see *E A* , pp 232 ff).
[16] Probably originally " there were in the world."
[17] L *three* (*years*), see *E A* , p 237.

offered in her [1]   46 And it came to pass after three thousand years [2] Solomon [3] built the city and offered therein offerings . then it was that the barren bare a son [4]   47 And whereas she told thee that she reared him †with labour†,[5] that is the dwelling of [6] Jerusalem   48 And whereas she said to thee My son entered into his (marriage) chamber and died [7]— this (was) the fall [and misfortune] [8] of Jerusalem 49. And [whereas] [9] thou hast seen her likeness,[10] how that she mourneth for her sons,[11] and thou didst begin to console her for what had befallen her [12]—

50. And now the Most High hath seen
   that thou art grieved with all thy soul,
   and with all thy heart sorrowest on her account .
   And he hath shewn thee the light of her glory,
   and the beauty of her loveliness.

51 Therefore I bade thee await me [13] in the field where no house hath been builded ,   52 for I knew

---

[1] Perhaps *in it* (the world) is the right text (see *E A* , p 237)—*in her* can only mean " in the heavenly Sion ", the earthly Jerusalem (= the " son " here) only became the Holy City when David instituted the sacrificial cultus in it, cf iii 24

[2] The 3000 years apparently represents the interval of time from the Creation to the founding of the Temple, according to the Hebrew text, see *E A* , p 238

[3] According to iii 24, David was the founder of the Holy City, perhaps *David* should be read here (see *E A* , p 238)

[4] i e the earthly Jerusalem probably

[5] So read (slightly emending text), text has *world*

[6] i e probably the Divine Presence (Shekinah) in the Temple, which was constantly interrupted by sin

[7] L + *and that misfortune befell her* (so Ar [1], cf also Ethiop)

[8] Added by Syriac (? part of the omitted previous clause) Note that the death of the son = the fall of the earthly Jerusalem (i e the son = the earthly Jerusalem)

[9] Lit *that* , perhaps to be omitted, otherwise the sentence has no conclusion

[10] i e probably the heavenly pattern of Sion (the heavenly Jerusalem), cf Heb xi 10, 16, xii 22, xiii 14

[11] So Ethiop , but the other Versions rightly *son*

[12] A gloss in L (some MSS) adds *these were the things to be opened unto thee*   the other Versions omit.

[13] L *remain.*

that the Most High was about to reveal all these things to thee   [53 Therefore I bade thee come into a place [1] where no foundation of a building is ,   54 for no work [2] of man could remain in the place where the City of the Most High was about to be revealed] [3] 55 But be not thou afraid, and let not thy heart be disquieted, but go in and see [4] the light of the glory [4] and the vastness of her building, as far as the sight of thine eyes alloweth [5] thee to see ,   56 and afterwards thou shalt hear as far as the hearing of thine ears alloweth [5] thee to hear [6]

57. For thou art blessed above many,
    and art named [7] before the Most High as (but) few ! [8]

Transition to the Fifth Vision (X. 58–59)

58. But on the night of to-morrow thou shalt remain here [9] ,   59 and the Most High will shew thee [10] a vision of those revelations [10] which the Most High will do to the inhabitants of the earth in the last days.

---

[1] L *the field*
[2] L *building-work*
[3] Vers 51–52 and 53–54 are doublets apparently, though all the Versions attest them , see *E ℔* , p 241
[4] L *the brightness*
[5] Lit sufficeth
[6] The seer saw and heard much more than is recorded , this implies a real experience   note that the City is regarded as still standing before the seer   with vers 55–56 cf 1 Cor. 11 9
[7] *i e* singled out by name for special honour
[8] The true sequel appears to be contained in xii, 39*b*, xiii 57–58 and xii 40–48 (see *E A* , p 242)
[9] *i e* in the field of Ardat
[10] L *those visions in dreams* (*i e* dream-visions) , cf Ethiop , the sense seems to require *in dream-visions*

VISION V

(THE EAGLE VISION)[1] (X. 60—XII 51)

The Vision (X 60—XII. 3a)

60. And I slept there [2] the next night as he commanded me

XI 1. And it came to pass in the second night I saw a vision [3] and lo! there came up out of the sea [4] an eagle [5] [that (was) very large in its size],[6] and he had twelve wings [7] and three heads [8] 2. And I saw, and lo! he spread his wings in [9] the whole earth, and all the winds of heaven blew on him,[10] and the clouds gathered together unto him. 3 And I saw that from his wings were born [11] wings small and little and petty [11] 4. But his heads were at rest; but the middle head was greater than these others; and yet it also was resting with them. 5 And I saw,

---

[1] This famous vision is directed against the Roman Empire symbolized by the Eagle

[2] L + *that night and*

[3] L *dream* (Ethiop *in a dream*), a dream-vision is meant.

[4] Cf Dan vii 3, Rev. xiii 1

[5] The eagle is a specially appropriate symbol of the Roman Empire whose military emblem was the eagle

[6] Absent from other Versions

[7] So all the Versions except L, which has *feathered wings* For the significance of these cf *E. A.*, p 261 f

[8] *i e* in the original form of the vision the three Flavian Emperors, Vespasian, Titus and Domitian

[9] So L and Ethiop, but Ar [2] Arm *over.*

[10] Cf xiii 3

[11] L *anti-wings and they became wings petty and small* other Versions *little wings* for *anti-wings;* apparently usurpers or military rivals of the Emperors are meant whose activity was short-lived

and lo ! the eagle commanded[1] his wings to reign
over the whole earth and over the inhabitants thereof 6 And I saw how there became subject to him
everything beneath the heavens, and not one thing
resisted [2] him of the creatures upon the earth 7 And
I saw, and lo ! the eagle rose upon his talons, and
emitted the voice [3] to his wings, and said to them :
[Go, rule over the whole earth ! 8 But now rest
ye],[4] and do not all wake [5] at once, but sleep each
one of you in his place, and wake [5] by times, [6]
9 but let the heads be preserved for the last !
10 And I saw that his voice did not proceed from
his heads, but from the midst of his body. 11 And
I numbered his little wings,[7] and they [also] [8] were
eight. 12 And I saw, and lo ! there arose on the
right side [9] one wing [10] and reigned over the whole
earth 13 And I saw [11] that its end came and it was
destroyed,[12] so that even its place was not known.[13]
And [I saw, and lo !] [14] the second wing [15] arose, and
it also ruled over the whole earth a long time,
14 and it came to pass when it had reigned, its
end came that it should be destroyed,[12] as the first.
15 And lo ! a voice was heard which said to it ·
16 Hear thou who for the whole of this time hast
held the earth, this [message] [16] I announce to thee
before thou shalt be destroyed [12] : 17. None of those

[1] L *flew with* (rightly)   [2] Or *gainsaid*
[3] *i e* uttered his voice (a Hebraism)
[4] Absent from the other Versions
[5] Or *watch* each wing (a pair of wings) is to be active for
a limited time, and in succession
[6] *i e* for successive limited periods
[7] L *anti-wings.*
[8] Added by Syriac, L *lo !*   [9] See *E A* , p 252
[10] Perhaps originally *one from the pairs of wings* see *E A* ,
p 252
[11] L *and it came to pass* (cf the other Versions).
[12] = ἀφανίζεσθαι, L *appeared no more* (R V)
[13] L and other versions *appeared no more* (was not visible)
[14] Absent from the other Versions
[15] = probably Augustus (the first wing or pair of wings =
Julius Cæsar)
[16] Added by Syriac

who (shall be) after thee shall hold (rule) as [1] the whole of this time,[2] yea, not as [1] the half of it ![3] 18 And [I saw, and lo '][4] the third wing arose and ruled, it also as [5] its former companions,[5] [over the whole earth] [6], and it also was destroyed [7] [as the preceding] [6] 19. And so it happened to all the wings that [8] each one of them [8] ruled and again were destroyed [7] 20 And I saw, and lo ! in time the little wings also arose on the right side, so that they might hold (rule over) [the earth],[9] and some of them held (rule), but were destroyed [7] suddenly · 21. and some of them arose, but did not hold the rule. 22. And I saw after this that his [10] twelve wings were destroyed,[7] and (also) two of the little wings , 23 and there was left nothing of the eagle's body save only the three heads that were at rest and six little wings 24 And I saw, and lo ! from the little wings two wings separated themselves, and [11] went and rose up [11] under the head [12] that was upon the right side , but four remained in their place 25 And I saw, and lo ! these [13] four little wings [13] thought to rise up and to hold the rule. 26 And I saw, and lo ! one rose up,[14] but immediately was destroyed, [7] 27 and again the second,[15] but it also was immediately destroyed [7] (more quickly) [16] than the first 28 And I saw, and lo ! the two [17] that remained of them

---

[1] = "anything like."

[2] L. *thy time* only (for *as the whole of this time*)

[3] The long reign of Augustus fits this description

[4] Absent from the other Versions

[5] L *the former* (cf Ethiop)

[6] Absent in L. and the other Versions

[7] See note [12] to ver 13 above

[8] L *one by one*   [9] Added by Syriac

[10] L *the*   [11] L *remained* , so Ethiop

[12] *i e* probably, according to the original meaning of the vision, Domitian who are represented by the two little wings it is difficult to say, see *E A* , p 255, for suggestions

[13] L *under-wings*.

[14] ? Galba   [15] ? Piso or Otho

[16] The comparative has accidentally fallen out of the Syriac text

[17] ? Civilis and Vitellius.

thought [of them][1] that they also should hold the
principate[2], 29 and while they were thinking [to
rule over the earth, I saw, and][3] lo ! one of the heads
which were at rest, the middle one,[4] awoke, and it
was greater than the two other heads   30 [. .][5]
the two [6]of them[6] with itself, 31 and [7] with the
two, that were with it, it turned and devoured
the two little wings[8] which thought to reign
32 But this head held (rule over) all the earth,
and oppressed[9] its inhabitants with much hardship, and wielded power[10] over the inhabited
world[11] more than all the wings that had been
33 And after this I saw, and lo ! suddenly[12] the
middle head was destroyed,[13] it also even as the
†wings†.[14] 34 But there remained two heads, (which)
also ruled over the whole earth, and over its inhabitants   35 And I saw, and lo ! the head which was
upon the right side devoured that upon the left.[15]
36 And I heard a voice which said to me · Look in
front of thee, [Ezra],[16] and see,[17] what thou seest [(at)
the end] ![18]   37. And I saw, and lo ! as it were a
lion that was roused out of the wood, [crying and][18]
roaring   And I heard how he uttered a man's voice
to[19] the eagle, and spake and said to him   38. Hear,
[thou eagle],[18] and I will talk[20] to thee . The Most High
saith to thee · 39 Art thou not it that art left of the

[1] Accidentally repeated from the previous clause
[2] L (cf Ethiop) *to reign*
[3] Absent in L and the other Versions
[4] ? Vespasian
[5] There is something missing here in the Syriac, L *and
I beheld how it allied*
[6] L *heads*   [7] L + *and lo ! the head*   [8] L *under-wings.*
[9] Lit *humbled*   [10] Or *prevailed*   [11] = ἡ οἰκουμένη
[12] So L , other Versions omit
[13] See note [12] on ver 13 above
[14] Syr text has *wing*
[15] i e Domitian (the right head) compassed the death of
Titus (the left head), as was popularly supposed at the time
see *E A* , p 157
[16] Absent from the other Versions
[17] L *consider*   [18] Peculiar to the Syriac
[19] Or *against*   [20] Lit *say*

four beasts [1] which I had made to reign over my
world, and that through them the end of the [2]
times might come ?   40 Thou, however, the fourth,
art come, and hast overcome all the beasts who are
past,

> and thou hast wielded power over the world
>   with great hardship,[3]
> and over the whole inhabited earth with [4] bitter
>   violence [4],
> and thou hast dwelt in the inhabited earth full
>   long with fraud,
> and hast judged the earth, (but) not with truth

42 For thou hast [5] plundered and robbed [5] the
>   [6] humble and true,[6]
> and evil entreated the meek [7],
> and hast hated the upright,[8]
> and loved the deceitful [9],
> and hast overthrown the strongholds of such as
>   were flourishing,[10]
> and laid low the walls of those who did thee no
>   harm—

43. And (so) thine insolence [11] hath ascended unto
>   the Most High,
> and . . [12] unto the Mighty One

44. And the Most High regarded his times,
> and lo ! they were ended [13],
> and his æons [14] were fulfilled [15]

---

[1] Cf Dan vii 3 , the eagle is identified with the fourth
beast of Dan vii

[2] L *my*   [3] L *terror (trembling)*

[4] L *grievous oppression*

[5] L *hast afflicted*   [6] L *meek*

[7] L *quiet* (or *peaceable*)

[8] L *them that speak truth*

[9] Or *liars* (? an allusion to Jewish informers)

[10] L *them that were fruitful* (i e prosperous)

[11] Or *insult*

[12] A word has fallen out accidentally in the Syriac, L
thy pride   cf for the whole ver Isa xxx 29

[13] The predetermined end has come

[14] = the word usually rendered *world* (αἰών)

[15] Cf. Gal iv. 4.

45 Therefore shalt thou be utterly destroyed,[1] thou
     eagle,
    and thy highest [2] wings,
    and thy [3] little and evil wings,[3]
    and thy bitter [4] heads,
    and thy evil talons,
    and thy whole [5] hateful and evil [5] body,
46 so that the whole earth may be rested and
relieved now that she hath been freed from [6] violence,
that she may hope for the judgement [7] and the mercy
of her Maker

XII. 1. And it came to pass when the lion had
spoken these words unto the eagle, 2 I saw, and lo !
the head that was left was destroyed [1] [suddenly] [8]
And then the two wings [9] which went over unto it
rose up in order to reign; and their principate had
an end [10] and was full of uproar   3a And I saw that
these also were destroyed [1] and the whole body of
the eagle was burnt; and the earth was greatly
amazed.

The Interpretation of the Vision (XII. 3b–39)

3b But I from great agitation [11] and much fear
awoke, and said to my spirit   4 Thou hast wrought
all these things unto me because thou searchest out
the ways of the Most High !
    5. And lo ! I am [12] enfeebled in my soul,[12]
        and my spirit [13] is much diminished,
nor is there left in me the least [14] strength because

[1] L *appear no more* (cf note on xi 13 above)
[2] As opposed to the *little wings* = L *horrible*
[3] L *little wings most evil*   [4] L *cruel*
[5] L *vain* (or *worthless*)   [6] L + *thy*
[7] Here *judgement* means the judicial process by which the
Roman Empire is destroyed, not the judgement of the last
day
    [8] Absent in the other Versions
    [9] So all the Versions (we should expect *little wings*)
[10] L *was short*   [11] L + *of mind*   cf x 28
[12] L *yet weary in my mind*   [13] L *in my spirit*
[14] Lit *not even a little.*

of the great fear which I have experienced[1] in this
night   6 And now I will petition the Most High, and
he will [2] strengthen me unto the end.   7 And I said :
O Lord, my Lord, if I have found favour in thy sight,
and if [3] in truth I have blessing (laid up) [3] with thee
above many, and if in very deed [4] my prayer hath
ascended before [the majesty of] [5] thy countenance—
8 strengthen me and make known to me, thy servant,
the interpretation and explanation of this [6] vision
that I have seen,[6] in order that thou mayest completely [7] comfort my soul !   9 For hast thou not
counted me worthy to reveal to me the consummation
of the times and the end of the periods ? [8]

10. And he answered and said to me   This is
the interpretation of the vision that thou hast seen :
11. The eagle whom thou sawest come up from the
sea—this is the fourth kingdom which appeared in
vision to thy brother Daniel [9],   12 but it was not
interpreted to him as I interpret (it) to thee now,
[10] or as I have interpreted (it) to thee [10]

13. Behold the days come when a kingdom shall
arise upon the earth, and it shall be more terrible
than all the kingdoms which have been before it.
14. And twelve kings shall reign in it, one after
another,[11]   15. But the second,[12] when he shall reign,
shall hold (the rule) a longer time than (any of)

---

[1] Lit *feared*   [2] L *that he may*   [3] L *I am justified*

[4] Lit *in truth* (but a different word from that used in the
previous part of the verse)

[5] Absent from the other Versions, cf vi 32

[6] L *fearful vision* (so Ethiop Ar [1]): *that I have seen* is
probably a corruption in Syriac of *fearful*

[7] This implies that partial consolation had already been
given (in the vision of the heavenly Sion), see *E A*, p 267

[8] See *E A*, p 267 f

[9] Cf Dan vii 7 f   This is an interesting case of re-inter-
pretation of prophecy , see *E A*, p 268

[10] ? an ancient gloss

[11] i e apparently the " twelve Cæsars," according to the
later (not the original) meaning of the vision, see *E A*,
p 268

[12] i e Augustus

the twelve   16 This is the interpretation of the
twelve wings which thou hast seen   17. And whereas
thou didst see [1] a voice which spake and did not
emerge from the head [2] of the eagle, but from the
midst of his body, this is the meaning [3]   18. (because) [4] in the midst of the time [5] of that kingdom
there shall be [6] many divisions,[6] and it shall be in
danger [7] of falling; and it shall not fall then, but
shall be re-established to its [8] former rule [8]   19 And
whereas thou didst see eight little wings [9] grow under
his wings, this is the meaning [3]   20 for there shall
arise in it eight kings whose times shall be swift and
whose periods hurried   21 and two [10] of them shall
perish when [11] the time shall come that divideth,[11] and
four shall be kept for the time when its time cometh
to be ended [12], but two shall be kept for the consummation   22. And whereas thou didst see in him
three heads resting, this is the meaning [3] ·   23. at
the end of the times the Most High will arouse three
kings [13], and they shall renew many things therein,
and shall grind [14] the earth   24. and its inhabitants
with much hardship, more than all those that were
before them.   Therefore are they called the heads
of the eagle ;   25. for these are they who shall renew [15]
his wickedness, and they shall consummate his end.

[1] So Ethiop Ar [1], but L Arm *hear*
[2] So Ethiop Ar [1], but L *heads*
[3] = οὗτός ἐστιν ὁ λόγος , cf X 40
[4] ὅτι (mistranslated)—here = *that*
[5] *i e* between Nero and Vespasian.
[6] L *no small contentions* Ethiop *much uproar*
[7] = κινδυνεύσει
[8] L *to its beginning* (= εἰς τὴν ἀρχὴν αὐτῆς), misunder-
standing Greek,
[9] L *under-wings.*
[10] *i e* in the last days of Nero, ? Vindex and Nymphidius
(see *E A* , p 270)
[11] L *the middle time approacheth*
[12] Cf *E A* , p 270
[13] So all the Versions except L which has *three kingdoms*
[14] Or *oppress* · L *bear rule over*
[15] = ἀνακαινώσουσιν, L *bring to a head* = ἀνατεφαλαιώσουσιν
which is right (Syriac misread) , see *E A* , p 271
G

26. And whereas thou didst see one great head destroyed [1]—(it is) because [2] only [3] one of them shall die upon his bed, but he also tormented [4], 27. but as for the two who are left, the sword shall devour them, 28. because the sword of the one [5] shall devour his companion [6], nevertheless he also shall fall by the sword at the end [7] 29 And whereas thou didst see two wings [8] go over unto the head on the right side, this is the meaning [9]. 30. These are they whom the Most High hath set apart for his [10] end, and their kingdom shall [11] have an end,[11] and it shall be full of uproar, as thou hast seen 31 And that thou didst see the lion that was roused out of the wood, crying and roaring and speaking to the eagle, and (that) he was reproving him for his iniquity, and all the [12] words,[13] as thou hast heard 32 this is the [14] Messiah whom the Most High hath kept for the consummation of the days, who shall spring from the seed of David,[14] and shall come and speak with them,

and he shall reprove them for their ungodliness,
and for their baseness admonish [15] them,
and set in order [16] before them their iniquity.

33 For he shall station them [17] before me [17] in their judgement,[18] alive, and it shall be when he rebuketh

[1] Cf note on xi 13 above
[2] = ὅτι introducing direct speech (misunderstood by the Syriac translator)
[3] Cf Ethiop, L omits
[4] ? Trajan (according to the later interpretation of the vision), see E A, p 271 f
[5] ? Hadrian
[6] ? Lusius Quietus (see E A, p 272)
[7] This seems to be pure prediction
[8] L under-wings   [9] Cf note [3] on ver 17 above
[10] i e the eagle's   [11] L be short   [12] L his
[13] = λόγων which may = deeds here, see E A, p 272
[14] Messiah   from seed of David cf Rev v 5, for the mixed representation (pre-existent yet born) cf E A, p 273, for the lacuna in L of this verse cf R V
[15] Or correct
[16] = ἐπιτάξει = L (infulciet) = ἐπιπλήξει, see E A, p 273
[17] Or fir t (different points) which = L.
[18] L in judgement.

them, then he shall destroy them [1] 34 But my
people who have been left he shall deliver in mercy,
(even) them who have remained [2] within my borders [3],
and he shall make them joyful until the consummation of [4] the Day of Judgement cometh concerning
which I have spoken with thee previously [5] 35 This
is the vision [6] thou hast seen, and this is its interpretation 36 And thou alone hast been found worthy
to have knowledge of the mystery of the Most High
37 Write therefore in a book all these things that
thou hast seen, and put them in a hidden place [7];
38 and teach them to the wise of thy people,[8] (even
to them) whose hearts thou knowest are able, com-
prehending,[9] to keep these mysteries

39a But do thou endure here yet seven days more,
that there may be revealed to thee what the Most
High willeth to reveal to thee !

Conclusion of the Vision (XII 39b–48)

39b And he departed from me
40 And it came to pass when [10] the people saw [11]
that seven days were past, and I not come [12] into
the city, all the people gathered themselves together,
from the small unto the great, [and arose] [13] and came
unto me and answered and said to me

41 how [14] have we sinned against thee,
or what evil have we done to thee,
that thou hast forsaken us and sittest in this place ?

---

[1] The godless are first rebuked, and then destroyed, see
E A , p 274
[2] L been saved   [3] i e within the Holy Land
[4] L even   [5] Or from the first
[6] L dream   cf xi 1
[7] Cf Dan xii 4, 9, 1 Enoch lxxxii 1, civ 11–13, and in
our Book xiv 26, 47, see E A , p 275
[8] i e for the circle of the initiated, the esoteric tradition
was preserved in secret
[9] L to comprehend and   [10] L + all
[11] L heard   [12] L returned
[13] Absent from L   [14] Lit what

42 For thou [1] art left to us of all the prophets
        as a cluster out of the vintage,[2]
        and as a light [3] in a dark place,[4]
        and as a haven of life to a ship when it
            standeth in a storm
43 Or are not the evils that have befallen us
sufficient [but that thou also shouldest forsake us] [5]?
44 But if thou forsake us, it had been well for us
if we also had been consumed in the burning of Sion !
45 For we are not better than those who perished
there   And I [6] wept with a loud voice [7]   46 And I
answered and said to them
        Be of good cheer, Israel,
        and be not sorrowful, House of Jacob
47.   For your remembrance is [8] with the Most High,
        and the Mighty One doth [9] not forget you for
            ever
48 But I have not forsaken you, and will not forsake [10]
you, but I have come to this place
        to pray for the devastation of Sion,
        and to ask mercy for our [11] Sanctuary's humilia-
            tion

Transition to the Sixth Vision (XII 49–51)

49 And now go ye every one to his own house and I
will come unto you [12] after these days [12]   50 And the
people went into the city as I had bidden them.
51. But I sat in the field [13] seven days as he had
commanded me , and I ate of the flowers of the field
only, and of the herbs was my food in those days

[1] Ethiop and some MSS of L + *alone* (but best MSS of
L omit)
[2] Cf ix 21 , Isa xvii 6, xxiv 13   [3] Or *lamp*
[4] Cf 2 Pet 1 19 (? a citation from our passage)
[5] This clause has accidentally dropped out of L
[6] So Ar [1], but L , Ethiop , Ar [2] have rightly *they* (Greek
ἔκλαιον can be translated either way)
[7] Cf *Ap Bar* xxxii 8   [8] Cf *E A* , p 279
[9] L *hath not forgotten*   [10] L *depart from*, so Ethiop Ar [1]
[11] L *your*   [12] Viz those mentioned in xii 39
[13] i e of Ardat (cf ch ix)

VISION VI

The Vision (XIII. 1-13*a*)

XIII 1. And it came to pass after seven days, and
[1] I saw a vision [1] in the night   2 and lo ! a great [2]
wind arose in [3] the sea, so that it stirred all its waves.
3 And I saw, [4] [and lo ! the wind brought up from
the heart of the sea as it were the form of a Man
And I saw, and lo !] [4] this man flew with the clouds
of heaven [5], and wherever he turned his face to
look [and see] [6] everything [7] before his look [7] trembled ,
4 and whithersoever the voice of his mouth went out,
all who heard his voice melted away as wax melteth
when [8] the fire causeth it to smell [8]   5   And after this
I saw, and lo ! there were gathered together a multitude of men innumerable, from the four winds of
heaven to fight with the Man who came up out of
the sea.   6 And I saw that he cut out for himself a
lofty [9] mountain and flew [and stood] [10] upon it [11]
7 But I sought to see the region or place whence
the mountain had been cut out, but could not.   8. And
after this I saw, and lo ! all who were gathered together to fight with him were in great fear, but yet

---

[1] L *I dreamed a dream ,* cf xi 1
[2] *i e* violent, L omits   [3] L *from*
[4] The bracketed words have been omitted in L by
homoioteleuton
[5] Cf Dan vii 13   [6] Absent from the other Versions
[7] L *seen under him*
[8] L *it feeleth the fire ,* for the figure cf Mic. 1 4 , Ps.
xcvii 5 , 1 Enoch 1 6 (of Theophanies).
[9] L *great*   [10] Absent from the other Versions.
[11] Cf (for the verse) Dan ii 45.

they dared to fight   9 And when he saw the violence [1]
[of the coming] [2] of their multitude that came, he
did not lift up his hand, neither did he hold spear
nor any of all the weapons of war,   10 but I saw
how he sent out of his mouth only as it were waves [3]
of fire, and out of his lips a breath of flame, and he
was shooting forth [4] glowing coals of storm [4]   11 And
these were all mingled together—the waves of fire,
and the breath of flame, and the mass [5] of the storm,
and they fell upon the violence [1] [of the coming] [2]
of [6] that multitudinous people [6] that was prepared to
fight, and burned them all up, so that suddenly
nothing was visible of that multitude of men without number save only dust of ashes and smell of
smoke   And I saw and was amazed

12   And after this I saw that Man come down from
the mountain, and he called unto him another multitude of men that was peaceable [7]   13a And there
drew nigh unto him the likeness [8] of many men,
but some of them were glad, and some sad, and
some of them were bound,[9] and some brought those
who were to be offered [10]

The Apocalyptist reflects on the Vision
(XIII 13b–24)

13b But I through great agitation awoke, and I
petitioned the Most High and said   14 Thou from

---

[1] = τὴν ὁρμήν (the assault)

[2] This appears to be redundant (see other Versions)

[3] R V flood

[4] L (corrected text) a storm of sparks   the whole picture
is based on Isa xl 4, cf Ps Sol xvii 27, 1 Enoch lxii 2
see E A , p 288 f

[5] So L : we should expect the same term here as that used
at the end of ver 10 (coals or sparks), see E A , p 289

[6] L the multitude

[7] i e Messiah's subjects who are gathered after the destruction of his enemies, cf Ps Sol xvii 27 f, and see E A ,
p 289

[8] L faces   [9] Heathen captives

[10] Returning Jewish exiles brought by the heathen as an
oblation, cf E A , p 290

the beginning hast shewn thy servant these wonders, and [while I am not worthy][1] thou hast esteemed me (worthy) to receive my petition [2] 15 and now reveal to me further the interpretation of this vision [3] ! 16 For as I think in my mind [4] · woe to those who are left in those days, and yet much more woe to those who are not left ! 17 Because (they) who are not left shall be grieved 18 over [5] that which is reserved for those who are left in the last days, but they do not attain thereto

19 To those also who survive therefore woe ! For they must see great perils with many distresses, as these visions [6] shew 20 But yet it is expedient [7] that one should stand in peril and come into these things than that he should pass away as a cloud from the world and not see what happeneth at the consummation of the times

21 And he answered and said to me I will both tell thee the interpretation of thy vision, and also will reveal [8] to thee concerning those about whom thou hast spoken 22 Whereas thou hast spoken concerning those who survive [and concerning those who do not survive] [9]—this is the meaning [10] .

23 He that endureth [11] danger in that time, he shall keep those who lie in danger, even such as have [12] works and faith [12] towards [the Most High and] [13] Mighty One 24 See,[14] therefore, that more blessing is given to those who shall have survived than to those who have died

---

[1] Absent from other Versions—the Syriac text may here be out of order
[2] Cf ix 24, 25   [3] L *dream*
[4] Notice the reflective tone of vers 16–20, and cf. *E A* , p 291
[5] L *knowing as they do*   [6] L *dreams*
[7] L *easier*   [8] L *open*
[9] So Ar [1] (cf Ethiop), but L accidentally omits
[10] Cf xii 17 note
[11] A misrendering by the Syriac, L rightly *he that bringeth the danger*, i e the Messiah
[12] Cf viii 33, ix 7
[13] Accidentally omitted by L.   [14] L *know.*

The Interpretation of the Vision (XIII. 25–53a)

25. But this is the interpretation [1] of thy [2] vision :
Whereas thou didst see a Man coming up from the
heart of the sea—   26 he it is whom the Most High
is keeping for long ages,[3] through whom [4] he will
deliver his creation, and he shall bring through [5]
those who are left   27 And whereas thou didst see
that from his mouth there issued [6] a breath of fire
and of storm,[6]   28. and that he did not hold [in his
hand] [7] spear or warlike weapon, and destroyed the
[8] massed coming [8] of that gathering which came to
wage war with him—this is the meaning [9] ·

29. Behold the days come, when the Most High
† is about † [10] to deliver them that are upon the earth,
30. great horror shall come upon the inhabitants of
the earth.   31 And they shall plan to fight one with
another, city with city, and place with place, and
people with people, and kingdom with kingdom [11]
32. And it shall be when these [12] signs shall come to
pass, of which I have previously told thee,[13] then shall
my Son be revealed [14] whom thou sawest as a man
coming up.   33. And when all the peoples hear his
voice they shall leave every one of them his place
and the warfare which is among them [15] ;   34 and there

---

[1] So all the Versions except L , which has *these are the inter-*
pretations
    [2] L *the*
    [3] Lit *for many times* · the reference is to the heavenly
pre-existent Messiah (the *Son of Man* of 1 Enoch xxxvi –lxx.)
    [4] i e through the Messiah, but L *which by his own self*
(i e the Most High himself), cf *E A* , p 293
    [5] L *order* (= διατάξει), Syriac may have read διάξει
    [6] L *wind and fire and storm*   [7] L omits
    [8] Lit *mass of the coming* · L *assault*
    [9] Cf xii 17 note
    [10] So read (*dĕʿāthîd*), Syriac text *will make ;* Versions
support correction
    [11] Cf Isa xix 2, Matt xxiv 7
    [12] L + *things shall happen and the*   [13] Cf ix 1.
    [14] Cf vii 28
    [15] L *they have one against another,*

THE APOCALYPSE OF EZRA 105

shall be gathered together men without number,[1]
as thou didst see that they desired to come and
wage war with that Man. 35 But he will stand upon
the top of Mount Sion[2], 36. and Sion shall come
and be revealed to all, prepared and builded,[3] as
thou didst see the mountain that was cut out without
hands. 37 But he, my Son, shall reprove those peoples
who are come for their ungodliness, which things[4]
are like unto a storm; 38 and shall set in order[5]
before them their wicked deeds and the torment
wherewith they are destined to be tormented, but
after this he[6] that was likened to a flame[6] shall
destroy them[7] without labour by the Law[8] of him
who[8] hath been likened unto fire

39 And whereas[9] he summoned and gathered unto
himself another[10] multitudinous mass[10] that was
peaceable[11] · 40 these are the nine and a half tribes,[12]
which were led captive out of their land in the days
of Josiah[13] the King, which (tribes) Salmanassar[14]
the King of the Assyrians led captive, and brought
them to the other side of the River [Euphrates][15],
and they were led captive to another land. 41 For

[1] i e the heathen hosts arrayed against the people of
God and led by Gog and Magog, the battle of Armageddon,
cf Ezek xxxviii.–ix., Rev xvi 16, and see *E A* , p 294 f
[2] Here identified with the mountain cut out without hands,
cf Ps ii 6, and see *E A* , p 295
[3] i e the heavenly Sion (in the previous verse the earthly
Sion is meant)
[4] i e the rebukes   [5] Cf. xii 32 note
[6] This clause is misplaced in Syriac, it should come at
end of previous verse (*which were likened*, etc), cf. L
[7] Cf *Ap Bar* lxxii 2 f , apparently all the heathen are
included in this multitude, see *E A* , p 296
[8] L *that* (i e. the Law, not the Lawgiver, is compared to
fire)
[9] L + *thou didst see that*
[10] L *multitude*   [11] Lit *of peace*
[12] So other Oriental Versions, but L *ten :* see *E A* , p 296
[13] A historical error. Hoshea was the name of the King
(cf 2 Kings xvii)
[14] Syr text *Salbanassar* (same mistake in text of *Ap Bar*
lxii 6)
[15] Absent from other Versions.

they [had deliberated among themselves and] [1] had
taken this counsel that they would leave the multitude of the peoples and go to an inner [2] region where
never the race of men had dwelt, 42 that there also
they might keep their Law which they had not kept
in their own land   43 And they entered in through
the narrow passages of the Euphrates   44 For the
Most High then wrought marvels [3] for them, for
he held back the sources [4] of the River until they had
all passed over,[5]   45 that they might proceed †to
the dry land† [6] It was a great way to go, a journey
of a year and a half, and that region was called
Arsaph,[7] [(at) the end of the world] [8]   46 And they
have dwelt there until the last time   And then [9]
when they are about to come again, 47 the Most
High will again hold back the sources [4] of the River
[Euphrates],[10] that they may be able to pass over
Therefore hast thou seen the multitude of men [11]
that was gathered together in peace   48 But they
also that are left from thy people [shall live],[10] they
who are found within my holy borders   49 And it
shall be when he shall destroy the multitude of the
peoples that are gathered together, he will protect
the people that remain, 50 and then will he shew
them many marvels

51 And I said further to him   O Lord my Lord,
make known to me this, wherefore I have seen the
Man to come up from the heart of the sea

52 And he answered and said to me   Just as one
hath not the power to search out [and find] [12] or to
know what is in the depths [13] of the sea, so can none

[1] L omits   [2] L *further*   [3] L *signs*
[4] Lit *outlets*   [5] Cf Josh iii 15
[6] So read (by a slight emendation)
[7] Ethiop *Asaph*   L correctly *Arzareth* (= 'eres 'ahereth,
"another land" of Deut xxix 25 f (Heb 24 f), see *E A*,
p 298)
[8] Peculiar to the Syriac
[9] So Ethiop, but L *now*
[10] Absent from the other Versions
[11] L *multitude*   [12] Absent in other Versions
[13] Other Versions (except Arm) have sing.

of those who are upon the earth see my Son or them that are with him,[1] except in that time in his day.[2]
53a This is the interpretation of the vision which thou hast seen.

Transition to the Seventh Vision (XIII 53b-58)

53b. Therefore there hath been revealed to thee these things, to thee alone,
54 because thou hast forsaken the things that are thine own,
    and hast devoted thyself to the things which are ours,[3]
    and hast searched out [4] the things of the Law [4]
55 For thy life thou hast directed in wisdom,
    and hast called discernment " my [5] mother "
56 Therefore have I shewed thee these things, for (there is) a reward with the Most High
And it shall be after three [6] days I will speak other things with thee, and will explain to thee [7] the last marvels [7]

57 And I went and walked in the field [8] much and praised [8] the Most High for the marvels which he had wrought at (different) times,[9] 58 and (because) he directeth the times and what cometh in the times. And I sat [10] there three days

[1] i e Messiah's companions ? cf vii 28 or possibly a host of angels, cf E A', p 300
[2] Cf Luke xvii 22
[3] L mine (possibly we ought so to read here)
[4] L my Law
[5] L thy, cf Prov vii 4
[6] L + more
[7] So Ar[1], but L things difficult and marvellous.
[8] L and praised much
[9] R V from time to time
[10] i e abode (a Hebraism)

VISION VII

(THE EZRA LEGEND) (Ch. XIV)

Ezra's Commission (XIV. 1–17)

XIV. 1 And it came to pass after this,[1] while I was sitting under an oak,[2] and lo ! a voice came out from a bush [3] opposite me, and answered and said to me : Ezra, Ezra ! And I said   Behold (here) am I ! [4]   And I rose upon my feet, and he said to me . 3 I did manifestly reveal myself from the bush, and talked with Moses when my people was enslaved in Egypt ,   4   and I sent him, and he [5] led my people out of Egypt [and brought them into the wilderness] [6] and led them up to [7] Mount Sinai , and I held him by me many days,

　　5　and explained to him many marvels,
　　　and made known to him the secrets of the
　　　times, and shewed him the consummation of
　　　the periods , [8]

and I said to him .   6. Of these words some [9] shalt thou keep secret, and some reveal.[9]

[1] L (Ar [1], Arm) *the third day*
[2] Some well-known oak (? near or in Jerusalem), cf *Ap Bar* vi 1, lxxvii 18, and see *E A* , p 307
[3] Cf Exod iii 4
[4] L + *Lord* (so Ar [2]), but other Versions omit
[5] So Ar [1], Ar [2] and some MSS of L , but other MSS and Ethiop and Arm , *I*
[6] So Ar [1], absent from other Versions
[7] Lit *caused them to ascend*
[8] *i e* the sacred eschatological tradition, which was associated with the name of Moses (cf the *Assumption of Moses*), see *E A* , p 308
[9] These clauses are inverted in the other Versions   the secret " words " = Apocalyptic tradition,   the published " words " = the Pentateuch (" Law of Moses ")

7 And now I do say to thee, ⌊Ezra⌋[1]. 8 The signs which I have shewed thee previously, and the visions which thou hast seen, and their interpretation which thou hast heard—lay them up in thine heart, [and hide them][1] 9 For thou shalt be taken up from men and shalt be henceforth with my Son, and with such as are like thee, until the times be ended

10 For the world hath lost its youth,[2]
and the times are nigh to old age[3] . . . .

13. Now, therefore, set in order thine house,[4]
and warn thy people,
and console their lowly ones,
[and instruct their wise],[5]
and give up henceforth[6] this life corruptible,

14 [7] And let go from thee the burden[8] of men,
and let go the thoughts of death,[7]
and cast off now the weak nature,
and lay aside these thoughts that oppress thee,
and hasten to remove[9] from these times!

15. [10] For the evils that thou hast seen, which have come to pass now—even worse than these shall yet happen after them[10] 16 For as the world diminisheth through old age, so evils multiply upon the inhabitants of the earth.

17 For truth withdraweth further off,
and falsehood approacheth,[11]
for already lo! there hasteneth to come the eagle that thou hast seen in vision.

---

[1] Added by Syriac
[2] Cf *Ap Bar* lxxxv 10, and in our Book v 50–55
[3] Lit *to be old* vers 11–12 are absent from Syriac and Arm, they may possibly be a later insertion, see *E A*, p 310, and cf R V
[4] *i e* the House of Israel
[5] So Oriental Versions, L omits
[6] Or *now*
[7] These clauses are thus transposed in the Syriac, other Versions invert, cf 2 Cor v 4
[8] L *burdens*   [9] Cf Isa lvii. 1
[10] L *for yet worse evils than those which thou hast seen happen shall be done hereafter* (R V)
[11] Cf vi 27, 28, vii. 24.

Ezra prays for Inspiration (XIV 18–26)

18. And I answered and said   Let me speak before
thee, Lord !   19 Behold, I go as thou hast commanded me, and will warn the people who exist,
those, however, who are yet to be born—who is to
warn them ?

20. For the world is set in darkness,
     and its inhabitants (are) without light [1]

21 For the Law is burnt,[2] and no one knoweth
the works that thou hast done,[3] or what thou art
about to do [4]   22 If, then, I have found favour
before thee, send into me, [Lord],[5] the Holy Spirit,
and I will write all that hath happened in the world,
from the beginning everything that hath been written
in thy Law,[6] that men may be enabled to find the
path,[7] and that they who would live at the last [8]
may [9] know the way [9]

23 And he answered and said to me   Go and
gather together thy people, and tell them not to seek
thee for forty days [10]   24 But do thou prepare for
thyself many writing-tablets, and take with thee
Seraia and Daria [11] and Shelemia, together with
Helkana and Shiel,[12] these five [13] men, because they
are equipped for writing quickly,   25 and thou shalt
come hither and I will light in thine heart a lamp of
discernment which shall not be extinguished until

[1] i e without the light of the Law, cf for the general
idea Ephes vi 12
[2] Cf iv 23
[3] i e the historical Books of the O T
[4] i e the eschatological parts of the O T
[5] Absent from the other Versions
[6] *Law* in the wide sense = the Holy Scriptures (of the
O T), see *E A* , p 313
[7] Ethiop + *of life* (a correct gloss)
[8] Cf *Ap Bar* lxxvi 5, for *life* = eternal life in such
contexts, cf *E A* , p 313
[9] L *live*
[10] Moses was in the mount 40 days (cf Exod xxxiv 28),
Ezra is the " second Moses "
[11] Read *Dabria* as in L.
[12] ? *Asihel*   [13] See *E A* , p 314

thou shalt complete what thou art about to write
26 And when thou shalt have finished, some of them
thou shalt make public,[1] and some thou shalt [2] conceal,
and shalt deliver them [2] to the wise, [for] [3] to-
morrow at this time thou shalt begin to write.

Ezra's Last Words (XIV. 27–36)

27 And I went, as he had commanded me, and
gathered together all the people, and said to them . [4]
28. Hear, Israel, these words   29 Our fathers were
formerly [5] strangers in the land of Egypt, and were
delivered from thence   30. And they received the
Law of life [6] and kept it not, which [7] you also after
them have transgressed   31 And a land was given
to you for an inheritance in the land of Sion, but you
and your fathers have committed iniquity and have
not kept the ways which [8] Moses, the servant of the
Lord [8] commanded you   32 But the Most High,
who is a judge of truth,[9] took from you [10] what for a
time [10] had been given to you   33 And now ye are
here in distress, and your brethren [11] are (further)
inland (removed) from you [11] in another land
34 If ye, then, will [12] admonish your soul,[12]
    and will discipline your heart,
    ye shall be preserved [13] in your life,[13]

---

[1] i e publish to all   [2] L deliver in secret
[3] Added by Syriac
[4] For the following cf Moses' farewell discourse in Deut
(chs xxvii.–xxxi)
[5] Or at the beginning
[6] i e which could win life and immortality for those who
observed it, cf ix 31 f
[7] So L (? read even as , see E A , p 316)
[8] L (Arm Ethiop) the Most High   the Syriac inserts the
Most High at the beginning of the following verse
[9] i e a true or faithful judge
[10] L in due time what   see E A , p 316
[11] Or are further inland than you (cf Ethiop) L are among
you (i e the Ten Tribes have already returned), see E A ,
p 316 f
[12] L rule over your understanding   [13] L alive

and after death mercy shall befall[1] you.
35. For judgement cometh after death,
    when we live again ;
    and then shall the name[2] of the righteous be
    revealed,
    and the works of the ungodly be made manifest.
36 But let none approach unto me nor seek me for
forty days.

The Restoration of the Scriptures (XIV. 37–48)

37 And I took these five man as he had commanded me, and went into the field, and we remained
there [as he had told me][3]   38 And it came to
pass on the morrow,[4] and lo ! a voice called to me,
and said :
        Ezra, [Ezra],[5] open thy mouth
        and drink what I give thee to drink !
39 And I opened my mouth and saw, (and lo !)
there came[6] to me a full cup, and it was full as it
were (of) water, and its appearance[7] was like fire.[8]
40 And I took and drank   And it came to pass
when I had drunk it, lo !
        My heart overflowed with discernment,
        and[9] my breast poured forth wisdom,[9]
        and my spirit retained memory[10]
41. And my mouth was opened and was not shut.
    42 But the Most High gave understanding to the
five men, and they wrote the things that were dic-

[1] Lit. *be upon*
[2] L *names*
[3] So Ar[2], the other Versions omit
[4] Lit *on the day of the morrow*
[5] So Ar[1], Ar[2] and Arm , but L and Ethiop omit
[6] L *was reached*
[7] Or *likeness*   L *colour*
[8] The cup is the cup of inspiration filled with the Holy
Spirit   the original inspiration of the Scriptures is here repeated , see *E A* , p 318
[9] L *wisdom grew in my breast*
[10] An interesting feature in this picture of inspiration , cf
E A , p 319

tated in order,[1] in written signs that they knew not.[2]
And I [3] sat there forty days, 43 but they wrote by
day, and at night did eat bread [alone] [4], I, however,
dictated by day, and at night was not silent [5] 44 And
in forty days were written ninety and four [6] books.
45 And it came to pass when the forty days were
completed, the Most High spake with me, and said
to me   The twenty and four books that ye [7] have
written [first],[8] make public that those who are worthy
and those who are not worthy [from (among) the
people] [9] may read therein [10] :   46. but the seventy [11]
thou shalt keep and deliver them to the wise of thy
people.   47 For in them are
> the veins [12] of understanding,
> and the fountains [13] of wisdom,
> and the †stream† [14] of knowledge
48. And I did so [15] in the seventh year, in the sixth
week, after five thousand years of the creation, and
three months and twelve days.[16]

[1] In unbroken succession (the root meaning of the word
used is *flow*)
[2] *i e* in the " square " Hebrew script used in printed
Hebrew of this which replaced the old Hebrew script Ezra
was regarded as the inventor, see *E A* , p 319
[3] So Arm (Ar [1]), but L Ethiop *we*
[4] Absent in other Versions
[5] Cf 2 Enoch xxiii 3 f (Vretil dictates, and Enoch writes
in 30 days and 30 nights 366 books)
[6] So the Oriental Versions rightly, L has 904 (and variants)
[7] L *thou (hast)*
[8] So all the Versions except L , which omits
[9] Added by Syriac
[10] The 24 books = the books of the O T , which was read
publicly in the synagogue, for the reckoning cf *E.A* ,
p 320
[11] L + *last*   the 70 books = the Apocalyptic literature
contained in secret books
[12] *i* **e** *springs*   L. has sing
[13] L. sing
[14] So read (by a slight emendation)
[15] Here text of L breaks off, the remaining verses are
preserved in the Oriental Versions
[16] = 5042 a m   See *E A* , p. 321.

H

Conclusion of the Book (XIV. 49–50)

49. And thereupon [1] was Ezra caught away and taken to the place of such as were like him,[2] after he had written all these things. 50. But he was called the [3] Scribe of the Knowledge of the Most High for ever and ever.[3] Ended is the first discourse of Ezra.

[1] Lit *in them* (the days mentioned)
[2] Cf vi. 26, vii 28, xiii. 52, xiv 9.
[3] Title of Enoch (cf 1 Enoch xii. 3 f , xv. 1), see *E.A.*, p. 321

APPENDIX

*Nor wilt thou wonder that not all the books have
reached us, which Solomon in his wisdom composed,
when thou hearest that not even the sacred books which
Moses wrote, nor even those of the prophets, have all
reached us, but portions only of these, those namely
which God gave to Ezra the priest to preserve and write,
and administer, that they might be handed down and
come to us, so that in them and from them we might
learn the knowledge of those things that are befitting.
But further, not even all those (writings) that Ezra wrote
have reached us, for of the ninety books which it is
written and alleged that he caused to be written, only
those which are read in Church have reached us.*

The above passage, which is extant at the end of
the 13th Epistle of Jacob of Edessa, was published
(in the Syriac text) by Dr William Wright in *The
Journal of Sacred Literature* for January 1867. Its
reference to our Book seems to be unique in Syriac
Literature so far as at present known. The last words
may possibly imply that 4 Ezra was one of the books
" which are read in Church," *i e.* in the Syrian
churches, but this is not certain. The number *ninety*
should be corrected to *ninety-four*